Transforming Trauma

Transforming Trauma

A Path toward Wholeness

Teresa Rhodes McGee

ORBIS BOOKS
Maryknoll, New York 10545

Founded in 1970, Orbis Books endeavors to publish works that enlighten the mind, nourish the spirit, and challenge the conscience. The publishing arm of the Maryknoll Fathers & Brothers, Orbis seeks to explore the global dimensions of the Christian faith and mission, to invite dialogue with diverse cultures and religious traditions, and to serve the cause of reconciliation and peace. The books published reflect the views of their authors and do not represent the official position of the Maryknoll Society. To learn more about Maryknoll and Orbis Books, please visit our website at www.maryknoll.org.

Library of Congress Cataloging-in-Publication Data

McGee, Teresa Rhodes.
  Transforming trauma : a path toward wholeness / Teresa Rhodes McGee.
    p. cm.
  ISBN-13: 978-1-57075-615-3 (pbk.)
  1. Suffering—Religious aspects—Suffering. 2. Psychic
trauma—Religious aspects—Christianity. I. Title.
  BV4909.M346 2005
  248.8'6—dc22
                              2005011569

*Human suffering, the sum total of suffering
poured out each moment over the whole earth,
is like an immeasurable ocean.
But what makes up this immensity?
Is it blackness; emptiness, barren wastes?
No, indeed: it is potential energy.*

Teilhard de Chardin
"Hymn of the Universe"

Contents

Acknowledgments   ix

Prologue   xi

Opening the Door   1

The Protection of Life   20

Natural Reactions   37

Living Memory   46

Waters of Grief   71

A Grief beyond Telling   91

Fire   98

Dry Bones   115

Narrative and Justice   130

Making Memorials   139

A New Heaven and a New Earth   149

Acknowledgments

The space and confidence to write is given to me by my husband, Richard, and our two sons, Michael and Patrick. Their encouragement is a part of the expression of love that brings joy into our lives. Michael Leach and the staff of Orbis Books have been patient while waiting for this manuscript to materialize. I thank them for their faith in me. The Rev. Gary Hellman and Dr. Mary Ragan, both of the Psychotherapy and Spirituality Institute in New York City, have been enormously helpful in the development of my understanding of trauma. Gary has been enlightening about linking spirituality and psychotherapy as a powerful resource for the healing of trauma survivors. Mary's insights on traumatic grief are greatly appreciated. The material was shaped by the feedback and experience of the students and staff of the Instituto de Idiomas in Cochabamba, Bolivia, who were participants in a workshop Mary and I did on Trauma and Spirituality. The Rev. Stephan Judd, Ph.D., and Sister Shu-Chen Wu, directors of the Institute, further contributed to the material by setting up opportunities to receive the stories of people who have worked in traumatic circumstances for a long time. Dr. Mary D'Arcy and Linda Unger were helpful in sorting out the meaning and patterns of these stories. The Rev. Hannah Andersen exposed me by concept and example to the rich tradition of Rahamin and shared her painting, "Woven Cross," for the book cover. Finally, I express gratitude to the people who day after day trust me with their tender hearts. Any examples used in this book have been altered to protect their trust.

Prologue

I am awed by the mystery that human suffering powerful enough to destroy life can also transform it. Those whose life experience is enough to leave anyone feeling broken beyond repair manage to have hope and an immeasurable depth of compassion for others. I have seen people garner the courage to place their deepest wounds at the service of the community. The survivors of sexual and domestic abuse, political violence, torture, and indiscriminate violence have stepped forward in their pain and called their experiences by name. People who have lost loved ones risk reawakening the rawness of their grief by becoming supportive of others who are bereaved. Recent history demonstrates that entire cultures subjected to the worst abuses imaginable have found hope for the future by honoring the memory of their past, daring to speak of reconciliation from the depths of their wound.

It is the wonder of that mystery that led me to begin the research for this book. As a spiritual director and as a human being, I needed to understand how to encourage the transformation of pain. How can it be that such bright sparks of hope are present in the stubble of human suffering? What is it in the human spirit that maintains hope, even when external and internal circumstances are deeply wounding? What is the process that makes the difference in whether people heal with a deeper sense of community or languish in the isolation of their pain? I began my exploration with a misplaced confidence that I would be able to actually articulate and place between two covers the answers to those ancient questions.

Like anyone foolish enough to try and understand a mystery, I soon learned that this is not a topic easily summarized and there is no one magic formula for healing. All writers must at some point look their original motives in the eye, make peace with their hubris, and surrender to the reality that, at best, the authentic book intended to help others is really a process of naming what the writer herself most wants to explore. And in this age when life seems so tenuous and the human wound so deep, I want not only to articulate something about the mystery of resilience and transformation but also to reflect on how life is constantly shaped and changed by our experience of traumatic suffering. I have found that I can best do that by looking at commonalities in the experience of those who have suffered and achieved a sense of wholeness without denying the reality of difficult experience.

Taken from the Greek *tramatos,* meaning an injury from an external source, trauma is the physical, spiritual, and emotional wound caused by circumstances that are, in some way, a threat to life. The traumatic wound touches all elements of our humanity in a way that leaves little doubt about the fact that we are one whole: mind, body, and spirit. The threat of physical death is only one possibility. Emotional abandonment is equally devastating, particularly when it happens early in life. A severed sense of connection with God can feel like spiritual annihilation. Betrayal of trust that leads to injury is a traumatic event. Trauma cannot begin to heal until safety is established, and only then as part of a lifelong process. Most life stories contain some trauma, if not one's own then the echo of a loved one's difficulties or, often enough, a previous generation's terror. It is helpful for people who are going through a process of recovering from trauma to know that confusing symptoms of trauma are actually normal responses to threat against life.

There is a substantial body of literature on the psychological and emotional treatment of people who have experienced trauma. The particular perspective that I bring to the exploration of trauma is that of a spiritual director. It is my sacred privilege to listen to others as they describe their struggle to integrate the experience of trauma with their spirituality. Since trauma frequently blocks styles of prayer and relaxation as well as the very possibility of connection with the sacred that has formed meaning in life, attention to spirituality is intrinsically part of healing any human wound.

Trauma changes our assumptions of identity, safety, and relationship with the world. Healing from trauma requires consciously knowing, as part of our life and self-concept, the unspeakable, the terrifying, and the incomprehensible realities of what people do to each other. Spirituality and trauma are both defining elements of our humanity. The response to traumatic circumstances is life preserving. It reflects the tenacity of human spirit and its powerful desire to survive in spite of threat and injury. Spirituality transforms the personal experience of trauma by bringing the personal wound into the light of God's own brokenness. The feminist insight that the personal is political has a corollary in both trauma and spirituality—the personal is communal.

Whatever the source of trauma, healing takes shape in the act of breaking out of isolation and connecting with other people and the deeper meanings of human experience.

From such connections emerge possibilities for transformation of individual and communal trauma. Those who study resilience in people and cultures that have suffered long-term trauma point out that a saving grace for victims is a cosmology and spirituality that place the experience of the trauma in a larger frame, approachable through the rituals and actions of daily life. Transformation of the trauma requires holding it in the presence of a larger experience of reality that captures the cyclic nature of trauma, its life-threatening origins, and its paradoxical truths. The same underlying human resilience that saves one's life (at the cost of a traumatic wound) becomes a passageway for new life. The suffering that can cause individual isolation and societal division can also become a point of compassionate communion.

This book is written for people who have experienced trauma, are presently in a process of healing, or accompanying others in their process of healing. It is not meant to replace professional help or be a treatment manual. I write for people like myself: non-professional counselors, spiritual directors, teachers, human resource professionals, nurses, hospice workers, relief workers, survivors of trauma, and the people who love them. In these pages I offer reflections on how trauma impacts our sense of meaning in life and how the recovery of meaning occurs through honoring the truth of what has happened, what has changed, and how we retain hope in the midst of struggle. My hope is that this book can serve to complement other processes of healing, including the invaluable resource of psychotherapy. I invite professionals who treat trauma survivors to reflect on the role of spirituality not only within the lives of their clients but as a personal resource in dealing with the vicarious trauma that all listeners suffer at one time or another.

I also write to provide a resource for those whose international experience has taught them that the whole of human suffering is, indeed, as immense as the ocean. I have the rich blessing of being able to travel internationally as part of my work. I meet people who have dedicated their lives to the service of the poor. I have marveled at the generosity of poor people who divide their share of bread with others, and so increase their joy. Yet what greater trauma exists than wondering from day to day how to feed oneself or one's children? Invariably these trips remind me that people who witness the trauma of others and try to alleviate it suffer themselves. It is difficult for missionaries, international aid workers, medical personnel, and anyone living or working in situations where there is so much pain to recognize that the suffering of others wounds them as well. However, we cannot become peacemakers without also listening to our own hearts. I sometimes must struggle mightily to remember this truth, because it calls me to recognize the difficult elements in all of our lives, especially when the temptation to deny personal trauma is always so strong within us.

There is a vital connection between how an individual recovers from trauma and the belief systems of the society or culture context in which that person lives. I believe that there is a great deal to be learned from cultures that have undertaken healing processes after devastating communal experience of trauma. These cultures teach us to use the whole of our lives as means of divine healing and love. The crafts, words, dances, prayers, stories, memorials, and courageous struggles for justice of those who will never have an opportunity for psychotherapy have a great deal to teach us about approaching our own wounds. Those involved with such undertakings as the Truth and Reconciliation Commission in South Africa and the REMHI project in Guatemala have transformed their experience of trauma from isolated suffering to a means of greater connection with the world. The process teaches that whether the suffering involves an individual or a collective trauma (and there is always a place where those two realities meet), peace is rooted in truth. Thus, I have chosen to draw from a few examples of communal healing processes around the world as a guide for the remembering and reverencing that are at the heart of human transformation. I weave the information about trauma through the warp of familiar stories and symbols: creation and exodus, body and spirit, the elements of life, and stories of people whose courage to live, even in the midst of inexplicable sorrows, gives us a glimpse of the face of God.

Opening the Door

Hᴇʀ ᴄʀɪᴇs ᴡᴏᴋᴇ ᴍᴇ ғʀᴏᴍ ᴀ sᴏᴜɴᴅ, ᴅʀᴇᴀᴍʟᴇss sʟᴇᴇᴘ. She was pounding on my front door, speaking Spanish, and begging for help. When I invited her into the house, she said between sobs, "No policia, no policia." I tried to pull words from my unused Spanish vocabulary to let her know she was safe. Then I just looked at her and heard the language of her body. She seemed folded into herself. Her blouse was torn and she could not stop crying. She had been through something terrible that no words in any language could adequately describe. There was only her body speaking its vulnerability.

I offered her something to drink. Slowly her story came out in the cadence of the terrified: words broken by sobs, each phrase followed by a plea—"Comprende?" She told me that she had recently moved from Mexico to Brooklyn. At the advice of someone in her neighborhood, the woman had traveled an hour and half to Westchester County, where I live, to buy a fake green card. She had been carrying all the cash she had. A taxi had dropped her off at a deserted parking lot near my home. The person she had met there took her into his car. He had no green card for her. He took all of her money, sexually assaulted her, and left her alone in the parking lot of a school. She ran for the nearest house with lights on, which happened to be mine.

My house is on a long driveway off a main road, tucked away and safe. Ours is a quiet neighborhood where incidents of violence are assumed to be miles away, in someone else's backyard. There are many houses closer to where the incident had occurred. Luckily, I had forgotten to turn off the porch lights before having gone to bed that night.

After hearing her story I made a few phone calls and arranged for her transportation back to Brooklyn. Then we sat down and waited. She was still stunned. To a lesser degree, I was too. I poured another Coke. She sat in her terror. There was no way I could blunt its edges. She begged me to accompany her to the taxi when it pulled into the driveway. I put on a coat and went into the November evening with her. I closed the taxi door and wished her well. Then she was gone.

My hold on consciousness was so fuzzy during the entire incident that the next morning I asked my family if I had dreamt it. No, I was told, the woman had been there. I found the Coke cans on the counter and remembered her weeping, distraught. When I reflected on her situation, I knew her fear—she had been betrayed and attacked. Being cast out of the country was too real a possibility to report the crime against her. She was profoundly vulnerable, and those responsible for protecting her had not been trustworthy. The woman had appeared at my door, calling to me from her terror in a language I could barely understand. She had roused me from a deep sleep and awakened the ghosts of my own fears—the knowledge of how easily and often women are assaulted and left to struggle on our own. This woman had experienced betrayal, sexual abuse, physical threat in a strange place, and found herself in need of mercy.

It was only when I told the story to a friend that I realized that letting a stranger into the house holds its own perils. In retrospect, I could imagine limitless dangers, all of which seemed very far removed from the vulnerable woman at my door. I wondered if I should have called the police, even if it meant the woman would have been deported. What were my responsibilities? When I answered the door, providing the woman with safety was the only thing that seemed to matter. I claim no courage in this story, because I was really not awake enough to make a reasoned decision. Perhaps my response was as simply as urgent as her need.

Letting her into my living room was one thing; the effect of her story on my heart was quite another. Sexual crimes are difficult to measure because, like the woman at my door, victims often do not report the crimes against them for fear of more violence. Estimates are that one in four women in the United States and one in eight men experience some form of sexual violence in their lives, many of them as children. Everyone's life is touched by this level of violation.

The Hebrew hospitality code articulated in the book of Leviticus speaks to the power of remembering the struggles of one's own people as a basis for behavior toward others. Be kind to the stranger in need, the Israelites, are told, as a remembrance that "once you were slaves in Egypt." The hope for the promised land is meaningless if not linked to the memory of slavery, exodus, and wandering in the desert.

Hope is born of the memory of God's fidelity. That memory is the basis for compassion toward others, an honoring of a personal and communal story that moves the heart. A refusal to open the door to this woman would have been a rejection of the memory of my life and the hope of my ancestors. Such an act would have been incompatible with life and the reality of deliverance.

SEVERAL MONTHS LATER, I reminded my husband to stop on the way home from work and pick up dog food. As he hurried out the door to catch his train into Manhattan, he said that he would never forget to feed a hungry beagle. I was home sick that day, overwhelmed by fatigue from rheumatoid arthritis. I tried to pick up my messages from the office but could not reach the voice mail system because a massive thunderstorm the previous evening had knocked out a transformer. The air was clear and fresh, the way it is after a storm strong enough to cause some minor damages. The beautiful day and my inability to reach my office seemed like encouragement to rest deeply, in body and spirit. I was grateful for the opportunity.

I had been sleeping long enough to be groggy when my husband's phone call came. "I am just calling you to tell you that I am all right." he said.

"Why wouldn't you be?" I asked.

"You haven't heard about the World Trade Center? Turn on the TV! I have to go into a management meeting about the evacuation, but I will keep in touch. We are a few blocks away and the streets are full of people. I'll call you back when I can. Don't wory, I'm all right."

I ran to the television set. The first station I tried was not broadcasting because its transmitter had been on top of one of the towers. I flicked through the channels and soon came upon the overwhelming images that have become embedded in the consciousness of the world, and sometimes still haunt my own restless dreams. While on one level it was all very vivid, on another, even with the distance of television, I could not take it in. I knew a number of people who worked very near the World Trade Center. I watched, numb with horror, as the first tower fell, and I wondered if my husband and other friends were on the street. There was no way of knowing. It was later said that the towers had fallen with such force that the impact measured the same as that of a nuclear explosion.

When my husband reached me on a landline phone, he said that it had become pitch dark. "There are so many people on the streets and now no one can see. I feel like I'm in a movie." That sentence has been repeated over and over by people going through experiences that are so powerful they take on an aura of unreality. The mind creates a merciful distance that preserves life. Survival requires disengaging—moving internally to a place from which the horrific reality can be "observed" more than experienced directly. Movies eventually end, but their most powerful images sometimes linger as after-images in the brain. So, too, with the terrible life events that we have survived through interior distancing: they live on in memory like violent movie scenes that are neither resolved nor ended.

As I watched and waited, I thought about Armageddon movies I had seen and of how, when they seemed to go on forever, I had wanted to forget the images and go home. The reality of the events on that day, however, did not allow for such an option. Reports came in about the Pentagon, the plane crash in Pennsylvania, the evacuation of buildings, rumors and conflicting information about how many were injured, how many planes were still in the air, and what would happen next. The safety of home was quickly being redefined, even as I called loved ones to tell them my husband was alive, but I had no idea how he was going to find his way back to our house. Much later I would meet a woman in Caracas, Venezuela, who said that, as she watched a live feed on television and saw the towers fall, her immediate thought was, "The world is coming to an end." In a very real way, the world that we thought we understood, with its safety and its assumptions, did indeed end that morning. It was a day of terrible trauma and profound solidarity.

September 11, 2001, was a turning point for the United States and the world. After that day, past, present, and future could not be understood or assumed in quite the same way. It was also a profound invitation for Americans to know the pain and the violence endured by the rest of the world. The terrorist attack on the United States opened the door to direct and profound understanding of vulnerability. The shock of those first days was permeated by a sense of mercy that often accompanies horrendous events. The world's first response was one of global solidarity and a tremendous outpouring of love and support. In the silence that followed something too horrible for words, there was a deep awareness of connection.

In terms of what it all meant, it is simply too soon to speak, too soon to understand, too soon to reach for the deeper implications of a future that would be so different. For all the words that have subsequently been written about September 11, 2001—including six hundred books published before the first anniversary of the attack—we have yet to fully grasp the significance and impact of what happened. One appropriation of meaning will never be sufficient; there will be an ongoing evolution of understanding as part of a living process.

Individuals and nations have long lived with memories of violence and the knowledge such memories bring; we are all vulnerable in what has become a dangerous world. The last conversation I had had with my husband that morning had been about dog food. Those words symbolize our common life; in the day-to-day of a loving relationship, we make quiet assumptions about the future. As I watched TV, I knew the rawness of discovering that the presumption of safety is sometimes downright arrogant. The future was suspended by the shocks of the moment.

My husband came home several hours later. His car pulled into the driveway like on any other day. He drove past the white pine trees in their quiet row. He parked the car in its familiar niche. When he stepped out of the car, I burst into the tears that I had held back all day. Perceiving myself to be calm under the circumstances, I had watched television and cleaned our house like a maniac, hoping that creating order around me would reverse the unfolding chaos. Through my vigil, I had known that Dick was alive. Holding him now, I began to appreciate the endless vigil of those who did not know if their loved ones were alive or dead. The unclaimed cars in the railroad parking lot that night offered the first clues of the losses yet to be realized. I could not imagine the pain.

When I hugged my husband, I smelled for the first time smoke from the fire that would burn for weeks. That smell hung over him, like it hung over lower Manhattan well into the nakedness of late autumn. While he took a shower, I scooped up the clothes and put them in the washing machine as if removing that smell from my house would make the whole devastating reality go away. It did not. The images of violence had come home. Things thought of as "over there" were now here. An artificial bubble of safety had burst, and its lingering impact could not be washed away in one cycle. Death had come as near as our noses, and though life was triumphant in our case, the smell of death reamined. It would come home on my husband's clothes for six weeks as the ruins continued to burn and the air held a lingering sorrow drawn in with each breath. The particles of that sorrow invaded the tender tissue of my husband's lungs as he breathed. He coughed for months. We knew by the sound of his wheezing that it was not safe to be taking in the air hanging over lower Manhattan. The air contained the toxic dust of the chemicals released in the fire, microscopic pieces of the asbestos used to fireproof the buildings, and unspeakably, the remnants of human life.

By January of 2002, three thousand different studies had been funded to follow the people who had been exposed to the disaster and its dust. Everything from the reading ability of then unborn children whose mothers had inhaled the swirling air of disaster to levels of stress hormones in relation to people's proximity to ground zero is being followed. The dust to which so many returned was mixed with the toxins released by the violence. It will be years before we fully know the extent of the injury carried by the air. The shadow of the dust will linger over all who breathed it into their bodies. Its power to destroy remains part of the ongoing violence unleashed that day.

Dust is often part of the life of those rendered powerless. The dust of powerlessness is the frailty of life, worn away one grain at a time, swirling in the unending dance of life and death, of helplessness and grace. No matter what efforts are made to contain it, the dust caused by violence takes a long time to disappear. Even then, its scars remain.

Sometimes people suffer so profoundly that deliverance must come from divine sources. The doors of churches, mosques, and temples all over the world were flung open to receive the terror and grief of those September days. Instinctively we knew that only God could hold something so horrendous and overwhelming, even as our prayer was deeper than words could express. I would begin to understand something of the power and complexity of that grief when I experienced the stunned silence in New York City a few days after the attack. Even the songbirds were mute. The faces of the missing were frozen in posters attached to any available surface. Details of where the person worked were printed in the hope that loved ones would be found alive. As the days went by, that hope grew dimmer, until finally the notion of "missing" settled into a lingering reality that made finding one small piece of a bone the focus of hope. Yet even that tiny shard of knowing was not possible for most. The medical examiner's office decided to carefully preserve material that might hold DNA with the hope that future technology may be able to identify elements of life that were left behind. With that, "missing" became "disappeared." When there are not even bones to bear witness, the rawness of ashes and dust create a void that will last for generations. Grief of that magnitude does not go away, even if buried below consciousness.

Like the rape victim who had appeared at my house months earlier, September 11, 2001, brought the sins of the world to our front door, bearing all the sadness of other losses of life and meaning and, in both an individual and a communal way, the loss of a sense of safety and self.

Makeshift shrines with candles and symbols sprang up all over New York City and the rest of the country. It was at one of those shrines that I discovered my own shadows of raw violence and hatred. The candles at the shrine had burned all night and left behind a multi-colored pool of wax, one long wick still sputtering. An Arab man stood next to me.

Believing that peace making starts in day-to-day living, I nodded and said "Good morning." Suddenly I was irrationally afraid and in touch with emotions that shocked and offended my own sensibilities. We were both standing in reverence and, while wishing for peace, I discovered in myself a blind rage that had little to do with the man himself. I felt rage at the order of the world, the failed expectations, the violence beyond control. Why was there not more safety in the world? And I knew in my heart that nourishing that rage would be easier than trying to learn a new way of living.

None of us is capable of only love and peace, none of us is beyond prejudice, violence, or reductionistic thoughts of revenge. In the fits and starts of terrible or terrorizing experience, we may think or act in ways that do not match our vision of ourselves. Good people are affected by the power of horrific events and sometimes behave in unthinkable ways. Waking up to powerlessness in the face of our own nightmares and contradictory feelings is sometimes the greatest loss of all. Embracing that loss is remembering again that we were once slaves in Egypt and that within ourselves we hold the potential to be our own cruel captors.

I wonder in the shadow of that captivity how we ever heal from wounds that seem beyond words, or for a time, irreconcilable with life. After the attack in the United States, there was a drive to experience what came to be called a new normal life. Consciousness needed to change for that new life to be a reconciling force. Such a shift involves more than getting the smell of the fire out of the house. It involves living with the knowledge that the world is not as one had perceived it and learning to accept that even when the vulnerability and grief in life can seem unbearable. Often after difficult experience there is a tremendous commitment and effort given to the notion of going forward, to returning to one's life as if the new reality is somehow not our life, to be brave in the carrying on of the ordinary. There is some wisdom in that approach.

Yet, like the woman at my door whose rape caused both of us to wake up the next morning with new knowledge, we all need to find a way of living in a world that suddenly feels dangerous in unimaginable ways. Those are the parameters of life after trauma of any kind, and they must be understood and appreciated. We return to the requirements of daily life to set a structure in place for the process of healing. We do the next logical thing. But it can be quite a fragile structure when our experience and expectations for safety in the world have been ruptured. The web of trust that holds life is torn by trauma, and it can take a long time before the threads are rewoven. In the meantime, there is suffering, anxiety, fear, and a loss of meaning.

If this is true of events that the whole world witnesses, how much more powerful is the breach of trust that is hidden and unacknowledged in a society? A few years after 9/11, when the color-coded terror alerts had become commonplace and the argument over how to commemorate the dead had been going on for some time, I visited Bolivia to do a series of workshops on trauma. Bolivia has a history of poverty, oppression, and political upheaval that dates back six centuries to the conquest by Spain. The native people of Bolivia were enslaved to do deadly work in mines that raped the earth, stole her natural riches, and killed the workers. The silver taken from Bolivia in the sixteenth century was enough to build a bridge back to Spain. Echoes of that exploitation reverberate in the urban migration, the drug traffic, and loss of identity that fuel street crime and drug use. Poverty creates trauma that is as unending as the struggle for life; it kills as consistently as bullets or bombs. The culture is wounded by pervasive suffering and grief. When life is continually threatened, as it is in most of the world, fatalism and rage are often the manifestations of the wound.

Several months before my visit, the president of Bolivia had entered into an agreement with a foreign company to sell expansive amounts of natural gas. Very little of the money from the sale would find its way back to the people of Bolivia. The natural gas was to be routed through a port in neighboring Chile that Bolivia had lost in the nineteenth-century war that had ultimately landlocked the country. Historic and contemporary trauma met in the response to the natural gas agreement. Like the mining of the silver and tin before it, the natural gas agreement would take from the sacred earth and give nothing in return. Old animosities with Chile were renewed. People called on the power of the wound left by the conquest to evoke resistance to another stealing of native riches. The president was overthrown because of the gas sale. The violence connected with the resistance to the agreement was serious enough to capture the attention of the international press, a rare event for a country whose struggles are usually invisible to the rest of the world.

I expected the focus of the trauma workshops in Bolivia to be the impact of the months leading to the overthrow and the violence of the overthrow itself. There was indeed a great deal of conversation about the collective trauma experienced in those historic moments. Then a bright young woman who works with a group trying to create a place of sanctuary for abused women and children said to me: "Of all that happens here, the greatest silences, the greatest sins are the things that happen in the home. No one talks about that trauma."

The silent wound that has no human witness or advocate is profoundly destructive, whether it is the wound of political torture or the wound of the child's unanswered cries in the night. Public sorrows are often reflected in private relationships; the violence that is seen has a hidden counterpart that lives close to home. Abandonment, domestic violence, and the impact of substance abuse are not restricted to one country or one household. A third of the people murdered in the United States are killed by family members or people with whom they have a personal relationship. We do not know the full extent of abuse against women and children because of its secret nature, but there is a growing awareness of the fact that such abuse occurs on a large scale across all social and ethnic lines. We do know that most reported sexual abuse against children is perpetrated by someone who is known to the child and the family. The images of that kind of horror live in individual, isolated recollections that, because of the fear they evoke, cannot surrender to the potential of healing.

LIFE IS FILLED WITH EXPERIENCES AND LOSSES that are traumatic for those who suffer them. A sudden, violent, or preventable physical death is traumatic for those left behind. The loss of an unborn child or of a child who dies at any age cuts to the heart of expectations about the future and the cycles of life. The wound is enormous. Any grief so powerful that one's emotional and spiritual connection with life becomes tenuous is traumatic. So is the loss of a meaningful relationship, a sense of unforgivable sin, or the fear of abandonment. Sexual, physical, and emotional abuse traumatize the victim. Life-threatening and chronic illness can shake the foundations of life, even for one who survives the illness itself. The actual outcome of events is less important than the perception or possibility of losing one's life at any or all levels.

The violence that we witness, the violence that we survive, traumatizes us. The loss of country, family, or culture is deeply wounding. The failure of institutions and structures to honor the faith placed in them causes experiences of betrayal and abandonment. Within six months of the fall of the towers, commerce and church were both shaken to their foundations. Pension plans that people had relied on to fund their future disappeared into the pockets of trustees. The revelation of tragic sins immobilized the Catholic Church at a time when stability was most needed. Some of the institutions that might have been turned to as a source of stability or comfort were unavailable and unreliable. The resulting sense of betrayal formed a trauma of its own. On the spiritual level, when one's relationship with God feels ruptured by difficult events, or the known access to the sacred becomes blocked, the result is a deep wound. When the God I have cried out to for help seems to fail me, the loneliness is devastating.

Many of the deepest human wounds fester in silence. The surprising things awakened by trauma find particular meaning in the realization that even our most private sorrows are part of the larger human story. Fundamental to healing is recognizing one's own humanity—including limits and terrors in the face of death—and seeing that through the wound, the world knocks on the gate of the heart. What comes to one of us eventually reaches us all. Pain held in a vacuum will never be able to be transformed. We who have the gift of loving each other can also inflict atrocities that reverberate for generations. It is tempting to keep that knowledge at a distance by focusing on the extraordinary nature of traumatic events, or to interpret traumatic experience only through the lens of personal shame. Yet, with minimal reflection, it is possible to recognize that huge issues of trauma and reconciliation connect us all.

Victims and perpetrators reside in the same households and neighborhoods. Entire societies and cultures live on the brutal edge of destructive economic and political systems. The trauma of globalization stills the soul's native dance, homogenizing the fundamental elements of human expression. Most of the people of the earth struggle each day for survival. Far from being what some literature refers to as "beyond the normal range of human experience," on a global level the trauma of poverty and horrific loss is part of everyday experience for the majority of the people of the world.

That reality speaks a challenge to the popular vocabulary of the weeks and months after 9/11. People spoke of needing closure so that their lives could go on, reflecting a perception that the wounds of violence can somehow be healed once and for all. There was talk of grief that led to anger and revenge and new divisions in the world. The sense of global solidarity faded quickly. The focus on the pain in the United States created a public attitude of "we" and "they," rather than a continued connection with the suffering of the whole world that stood in silence as a prayer for peace after the attack. The perception that people could be "made whole" through litigation and financial settlements was articulated in references to both 9/11 and the sexual abuse scandal that unfolded in the Catholic Church.

When lives are lost or destroyed in numbers and in ways unanticipated, becoming functional once again or being compensated can be confused with healing. While making restitution is an important piece of justice making, the process of becoming whole is not achieved by signing papers and prematurely declaring closure. When the intensity of the wound is experienced again, with all of its confusion and fear, the pain becomes a formidable enemy. We do violence to ourselves when we try to speed along or declare finished a process of transformation that has a life of its own. Disappointment that the pain from trauma doesn't seem to end—in spite of our commands—can make us feel inadequate because we lack control over our feelings.

THROUGH THE PROCESS OF LIVING through ordinary days and nights, I have come to believe that we can be healed from overwhelming events only by embracing the nature of our wounds in a context that is deep enough to hold the mysteries of life and death, grief and hope, compassion and rage. Healing from trauma is as multi-dimensional as the wound itself. Primary are the physical, psychological, and emotional aspects to the wound that must be addressed by the professionals in each sphere. Medical care, including the use of medication, may be needed. The sorrows that must be verbalized, the muscles holding pain and tension that must be relaxed, cognitive assumptions about what happened that must be corrected—all require a long process.

For healing to take transforming root, there needs to be enough support to hold the wound and check its tendency and the temptation to diminish vitality. The loss of hope is not simply pessimism about the future, it is a sense of abandonment and loss of connections in the present. Only the pain is real and it feels like it will go on forever; the dust of its ashes hangs in the air and damages the ability to breathe. Rebuilding hope through accepting the transforming power of compassionate relationships is both the process and the meaning of healing from trauma. The people in many communities who planted autumn bulbs in October of 2001 to commemorate the dead did so in the firm belief that life would bloom again in the spring. Months later, the bright colors affirmed their faith with a living memorial.

Whatever elements of healing are required, the making of meaning is fundamentally a spiritual process. Spirituality is the basis for living that consciously celebrates and gives expression to the soul and its ability to experience divine compassion. Spirituality is an expression of hope as it is biblically portrayed—a belief in the presence and fidelity of God that springs from living memory. It is the link between our deep rootedness in the divine and our human experience. Spirituality brings body and soul together, often in tactile ways like storytelling, music, dance, and consciously remembering the broader story of the human search for God. Spirituality is an active nurturance of the soul that is consciously renewed in the experience of daily life. We know our spirituality when we are struck by the beauty of something ordinarily taken for granted—the shifting cycles of the moon or the exact color of a loved one's eyes—that causes us to recognize God's artistry. Spirituality is relational; it is a process of making meaningful connection. Our spirituality gives us the desire to comfort the afflicted and celebrate new life. It is the source of our sexuality, our life energy naturally yearning for communion with the other. Spirituality is at the heart of human resilience and hope.

Transforming trauma is movement from the desire to inflict violence on others through retribution to those who have hurt us, or to ourselves for not having responded differently, to a reclamation of voice, hope, and imagination. It is impossible to make that transition without spirituality—a belief in something more than what is currently seen or understood.

Trauma disrupts and ruptures our previous understanding of life. Our journey toward healing requires a new vision that both knows the depth of the wound and has witnessed the possibility for hope. It was that type of transformation that guided the journey for liberation in a promised land. Healing from individual and communal trauma requires being held by an experience of God that is deeper than the pain. Yet this can seem like an impossible task in the face of life's betrayal.

- How do we pray or feel ourselves in God's presence when one of the fundamental elements of trauma is that trust has been ruptured?

- How do we make a reconnection with the God who knows our story, holds the memory, and gives us the gift of hope and belief in the future?

- How does the hollowness of trauma become the hallowed ground where we meet God in a transforming way?

These questions take on particular significance if religious language, institutions, or justifications are part of the infliction of the wound. The linking of religious principle to child abuse through destructive use of the rod, and the invoking of obedience to religious authority during an act of domestic or sexual abuse are particularly devastating. Violence done in the name of God—be it personal, or national, or international—is deeply destructive because it corrupts and betrays the language of the soul. People are often pressed to forgive before they have caught their breath; the lingering trauma then becomes framed as a religious or spiritual failure. That dynamic is at work when a rape victim finds herself at odds with her belief that forgiveness is at the heart of salvation. The inability to spontaneously forgive those who have trespassed against us in the most egregious ways easily deepens the shame caused by the trauma itself.

To make meaning of trauma is to reach beyond isolation and make a connection with the world. That is the power of spirituality—it links us to one another and to God. There we find love that nurtures life, even in the face of death. The knowledge of that presence is at the heart of healing and transformation; it is the experience of divine compassion that teaches us how to care for one another in the experience of the devastating and inexplicable. Unless we make a conscious connection to that care from and to others, the desolation of trauma can strip it of significance as a witness to the power and meaning of life itself.

The Protection of Life

LIFE HAS A STRONG DESIRE TO PRESERVE ITSELF. The earth has mechanisms of protection and balance that work to heal its wounds. Rivers pass through marshlands that clean them. Salmon struggle against strong currents to return to the place of their origin, spawn a new generation, and die within three feet of their birthplace. Birds know where to fly to escape life-threatening cold; they know when to begin their flight and when to return in the spring. Trees, plants, and flowers grow best in their native zones. The seeds know where they must be planted. They are part of the delicate system that creates beauty, sweet honey, and oxygen. The Hudson River estuary carries Atlantic salt a hundred miles north of New York Harbor. The ebb and flow of the tidal river nourishes life and becomes a meeting place of fresh water and the sea. The river is home for species of plants that must have exactly those conditions to flourish.

The power of flowers to break through a hardened lava flow shows the strength of the life force. Winds clean the air and bring new life, even in the face of assault. Animals are camouflaged to keep them from being destroyed by other species, thus preserving diversity and safeguarding the viability of the food chain. Life depends upon both built-in mechanisms for self-preservation and the ability to return to a balanced state when the threat has passed. All forms of life have the capacity to respond and adapt in different circumstances. Healthy life requires that the cycles of birth, life, and death be respected and allowed to follow their rhythm. Through this process, the earth changes and takes form, each response and adaptation having its place in the ongoing process of creation within which mountains as formidable as the Andes are still considered young.

All human beings are endowed with impressive life-preserving responses that affect every cell and organ in the body. Primary among these is the set of physiological responses that occur when the body perceives that something threatening is taking place, or is about to occur. That set of responses is automatic and without conscious control. It originates in the base of the brain, the part nearest to the spinal cord. That section of the brain is called the hippocampus, and it has primal origins. Finely tuned for the survival of the whole organism, the hippocampus orchestrates the release of hormones that quicken the heart, make the breathing more shallow, change the pattern of circulation, and heighten the senses so that the person can fight, take flight, or freeze in the situation. The body goes into overdrive, a hyper-aroused state that creates the energy for survival. Sometimes extraordinary strength is available because of an "adrenaline rush" that provides energy for the fight. This is the physiological experience that is known as stress. It is a response that has allowed us to survive as a species.

Stress mobilizes the system to deal with life circumstances that arouse emotion and alert the primitive part of the brain to the potential for danger. The stress response heightens the senses to obtain further information about the perceived threat and prepare the body for action. Stress is arousal of the body, mind, and spirit as a result of a demand on the system, a demand that can originate from both positive and negative situations. Some stress is a necessary part of being alive. Without the ability to experience the stress response, our bodies could not survive even the smallest of injuries. The powerful messages and physiological changes caused by the stress response are so complete and so potentially life saving that they govern even the clotting of blood cells at the site of a wound. This service to life does not request permission from the more rational, intellectual centers of the brain. It simply leaps into action to get us out of harm's way, involving every cell of the body as part of the process.

Ordinarily, once the danger has passed, the level of the hormone—cortisol—that activates the stress response precipitously drops. The heart rate slows, breathing relaxes, and the body is no longer aroused against a threat. Stress becomes problematic when the fight or flight response does not reach resolution. In such a case, the body remains aroused for survival even though the circumstances that provoked the original response have changed. When the body continues to be mobilized as if to fight something off or run from it, the life-saving response that was needed in the face of danger becomes damaging.

Unresolved and chronic stress can turn a life-preserving biological state into one that is life-threatening on the emotional, physical, and spiritual levels. To be in a chronic state of stress is to live in a body that is prepared to fight to the death over anything that challenges it, no matter how insignificant the challenge may seem to others. The physiological response cannot initially differentiate the level of danger posed by a situation; it is simply the body's answer to circumstances that are perceived as threatening. The paradox of stress is that its life-saving, protective capability is lost if the stress is not resolved. The body is aroused in a way that interrupts the usual flow of life.

Stress tends to be cumulative; small and large stress collects in the body. The unresolved stress from yesterday becomes more powerful when it meets new stress today. Very stressful events that are unresolved tend to create more stress because, in effect, all issues or challenges in life are experienced as having the same importance. The continuing physiological push for survival leads to a loss of perception about what is really important. That combination overwhelms the ability to prioritize or maintain perspective. The power of the stress response becomes the means of interpreting the world; waiting in traffic is transformed from a minor frustration to a circumstance worthy of a fight or flight response. When the arousal of the system for survival becomes a steady state affecting mind, body, and spirit, it creates new and paradoxical dangers.

We know the signs of stress in our day-to-day lives. It shows in the sudden anxiety and impatience we feel when another driver makes a mistake we take personally. Everything in life becomes more difficult. We may anger quickly or fear being overwhelmed by circumstances or our emotional responses to life. Reactions that exceed the seriousness of the precipitating event lead others to ask, "What was that all about?"—and often we do not know. The loss of perspective can occur so long after the initial source of danger has passed that it is difficult to connect it with the ongoing stress. A split occurs between the cause of the stress and its effects. We project the cause of the stress onto other objects, people, and experiences that may be in fact unrelated to the original stressors. The loss of connection between what initiated the stress and its continuation can make its causes more difficulty to identify and deepen the sense of losing control.

When stress continues, its life-saving capacity begins to threaten survival. The blood that thickens in anticipation of needing to clot a wound and save life can also clog the arteries of the heart and cause death, particularly if there is an underlying genetic susceptibility to such illness. Prolonged stress causes fatigue, muscle tightness, and headaches. There is a physiological basis for idioms such as "that was a real pain in the neck" or "the thought of it makes me sick." Unresolved stress induces exhaustion that is hard to address, because the body simply cannot relax and heal its wounds. Sleep may become difficult or non-restorative. Long-term stress makes people more prone to illness because the state of arousal impacts the immune system. Research indicates that stress is a component in most illness. At the same time, illness itself—particularly if it is a chronic condition or one that cannot be quickly healed—can cause stress.

It is tempting to attribute all illness to stress. However, that is not only an oversimplification; it runs the risk of blaming victims of illness for their symptoms. The relationship between stress and illness is best understood as a complex and cyclical interaction. We do know that illness is not wholly determined and defined by genetic markers or by stress. The role of pathogens seems to be mediated by a number of factors, including nutrition, underlying disease, and immune system responses. Nonetheless, the link between illness and stress is an important one. The role of stress in triggering illness for which there is an underlying genetic predisposition is being studied as part of the research into a number of diseases, including autoimmune disorders, cancer, and heart disease.

Stress causes behavioral changes. Eating patterns are altered; a loss of appetite or overeating can both be attempts at restoring the balance upset by stress. Continued high levels of cortisol impact the body in a number of other ways, including the way the brain functions. People under stress may have emotional outbursts that can be quite confusing and off-putting to other people. Emotional and physical withdrawal from others is a sign of not having the resources to maintain interpersonal relationships. It is not coincidental that these symptoms of stress can begin to sound like the symptoms of clinical depression and, as with other diseases, the depression itself increases stress. The interrelationship of chronic stress and depression is not surprising given the biological components of both; some of the same chemical messengers of the brain are involved in depression, stress, and the transmission of pain. Stress can impair memory and concentration, leading to a sense of distress at the fact that even one's mind is not working as well as it should.

Stress occurs in the body, but it can be fueled by unrealistic expectations of self or others. If one needs to be all things to all people, the fear of failure and its inevitable occurrence provokes a stress response. Perfection as a goal guarantees failure. The threat of losing one's identity or sense of self if certain expectations are not met reveals core beliefs not only about one's place in the world but also about the fundamental requirements for being loved. Distortions in those beliefs create even greater loss of perspective about the meaning of daily events. Stress can be caused by external circumstances that are difficult to resolve, such as the demands placed on the body by responsibilities to family and job, a chronic illness, financial threat, or the exhaustion of caring for another person. All of the inner resources of an individual under prolonged stress are mobilized for survival. Little else can be expected or accomplished. The continual stress of living in a situation of poverty, illness, violence, or uncertainty can result in what others see as an attitude of fatalism or hopelessness. The adaptation to relentless stress is frequently a loss of imagination about the future. Creativity suffers when survival becomes paramount; the body must tend first to staying alive. Stress has a way of making us focus on the present, because we feel under siege. That is the nature of its protective role.

IT IS TEMPTING TO MEDICATE the body's hyper-arousal with alcohol or drugs, or try to address the problem with hyperactivity, which stimulates the release of even more adrenaline. Yet true resolution of stress requires interventions that will not cause further harm.

When the workday ends, I am frazzled. There are heavy issues on my mind, problems that can't be solved, goals unaccomplished, the human condition a bit too close for comfort. I want to sleep or eat cookies. Instead, I drag my body to the pool, in no small part to avoid feeling guilty about the cost of the monthly membership. I remind myself as I put on my goggles that the water is cold and that I am too tired to swim.

The first few lengths of the pool are difficult. I am cold and cranky. Slowly, I stop fighting the water and I let it hold me. I count the laps. There is grace in the rhythm of the swimming. Over and over, energy is expressed and transformed. My body remembers all of its other swims. I learn again that to shift from a state of stress requires physical as well as emotional movement. I leave the pool healed from the day. The stress hormones bind to the oxygen I take in as I inhale and they leave my body as I exhale. The water I drink after I leave the pool washes away residual hormones that have done their job. I decide to forgo the cookies.

Every trip to the pool is a decision to preserve life by restoring balance to my body. I must make that same decision repeatedly, and against resistance. No matter how much I know about the theory of stress, it becomes embodied only when I actually get in the pool and allow the potential energy of the stress to be transformed in service of life.

The relief of stress is, like the stress response itself, a living process. The actions taken to reduce stress let the body heal. The danger has passed. We have the resources necessary to live and thrive in the world, but those gifts need to be carefully tended to remain in balance. That balance is the foundation for healing each day's injuries as we experience them, reversing the potential for danger into a proclamation of life. Then we will be able to approach a shift in core beliefs: to distinguish between the possible and the unrealistic expectations of ourselves and the world, to forgive ourselves for what we cannot accomplish, and to honor reality by tending the limitations and potential of our body.

The wound that is called trauma results from extreme experiences of the stress response. The same physiological elements are at work in traumatic situations, albeit in a heightened way. What separates trauma from the stress of an ordinary bad day is that trauma arises from a sense of powerlessness or helplessness over outcomes. The threat to life is experienced in a way that is more explicit, and usually more truly dangerous, than ordinary stressors. And there is nothing that the person can do to stop it. Trauma is often defined as an ordinary response to extraordinarily difficult circumstances.

One of the greatest obstacles to healing from trauma is the feeling that one is somehow culpable for what happened because of a failure to act in a rational, understandable way. Guilt about survival is common in circumstances where others have died. "Why not me?" can easily become as haunting a question as "Why me?" The feeling that others might have been saved if a different action had been taken, or if one had not acted in the interest of one's own survival, runs counter to the reality that the trauma response is not rational or planned in advance. At the heart of trauma is powerlessness—an inability to change the outcome of events for oneself or for other people. It is the very lack of opportunity to take effective action that defines trauma. The first act in recovering from trauma is often the recognition that a normal reaction to unusual events is not a source of shame.

During the first months of the war in Iraq, a young soldier came into a village where people had been killed in an explosion. Bodies had been blown to pieces. The horrific sight caused him to freeze and then experience profound anxiety that made him stop and throw up rather than follow orders and continue shooting in the direction of "the enemy." He experienced an anxiety attack in the presence of brutal violence. Some soldiers around him laughed at the bodies—which was a different but related response to the trauma. The laughing soldiers did what had been defined as their duty with an inappropriate affect that was provoked by the violent scene. They laughed as they shot. The soldier who experienced the anxiety attack and the ones who laughed both had predictable reactions to a horrible situation. However, the man who suffered the anxiety attack was recalled from Iraq to face court martial for the crime of cowardice.

A *New York Times* article about the incident caused an outcry. The reaction of the solider was more commonly understood than the Army had expected. Many a brave soldier revealed that he or she had experienced anxiety appropriate to combat situations, vomited at the sight of wounded and dismembered people, and had empathy for the young solider. The charge against the soldier was reduced to dereliction of duty. While he was charged with an offense that was less serious than cowardice and that merited a lesser penalty, this young man, who experienced a normal reaction under fire, was branded a failure.

Those who have suffered the horrors of modern wars have experienced loss of feeling, withdrawal from reality, depression, and rage. Such reactions have been experienced throughout human history, both by males whose trauma may have been battlefield related and by females abused in a variety of circumstances.

The observable signs and symptoms of trauma are at least as old as Homer's descriptions of the insomnia, flashbacks, nightmares, and headaches of Trojan War veterans. Those ancient soldiers experienced intrusive symptoms that made them feel as though they were reliving past experiences in the present. Restriction of emotion, hyper-vigilance in an effort to protect oneself from the past danger, and sometimes violent acting out of the original trauma are common in the ancient narratives.

It would take thousands of years for the symptoms Homer described to become part of a codified diagnosis for Post Traumatic Stress Disorder. Diaries written after many wars indicate that those who did "their duty" were haunted by traumatic symptoms. Doctors working in the U.S. Civil War documented something they called "Da Costa's Syndrome," a series of symptoms afflicting soldiers in combat.

When the ravages of World War I led to an increased incidence of the cluster of symptoms then known as battle fatigue, doctors noted that the soldiers exhibited symptoms exactly like those of the female "hysterics" living in psychiatric institutions. Indeed, survivors of war, like survivors of domestic abuse, described a loss of trust in the goodness of humanity, depression, problems with substance abuse, and a changed sense of identity.

Although the connection between symptoms of trauma experienced by men on the battlefield and the "hysterical" reaction of women whose experience of violence was usually in the "safety" of their homes was noted, it unfortunately did not lead to validation of the suffering of the women or the men. Rather, it was seen as further evidence of loss of manhood demonstrated by the afflicted soldiers in their cowardice and failure. The men had become like hysterical women, an observation that simply deepened their sense of dishonor.

SIGMUND FREUD ORIGINALLY BELIEVED that trauma was at the heart of all mental illness. Most of his patients were veterans of private battlefields. Freud's patients described to him trauma that often originated in physical, emotional, and sexual abuse at the hands of their caretakers. Freud is thought to have been unable to believe that the molestation of children occurred at the rate his practice seemed to indicate. The only way to reconcile what he heard in the consulting room with his own belief about the culture in which he lived was to decide that the trauma described by his patients was the result of their own childhood sexual desires and fantasies. Freud changed his focus to the internal psychic process as the root of neurosis and psychosis. Treatment, then, came to reside in the working through of the conflicts created by these fantasies produced by the id and moderated by the ego and superego in a neurotic way.

Other psychiatrists of the era, however, maintained their belief in trauma as a causal factor in emotional suffering. Pierre Janet, a contemporary of Sigmund Freud, worked with the women institutionalized at Salpaetriere, the same Paris hospital where Princess Diana would die a century later. In Dr. Janet's time, it was known as the Hospital for Hysterics. His patients suffered a range of symptoms, including expression of intense emotion, states of terror and a feeling of disembodiment, anxiety and flashbacks. These women were considered to be hopelessly beyond the range of normal human behavior. Dr. Janet believed that their symptoms were connected to trauma caused by actual circumstances and experiences and, as such, were normal human responses to reality. He conducted research on the physical and emotional reality of the women and developed treatment methods that have found remarkable resonance in the twenty-first century.

Like Freud, Pierre Janet listened carefully to his patients. Janet, however, believed their stories of abuse, isolation, mistreatment, and violence. He encouraged his patients to tell their stories, even when the narrative seemed incoherent. He learned that talking about the reality of experience in a supportive environment helped heal the trauma of his patients. Dr. Janet encouraged them to know and tell their stories, fitting together pieces of experience in a narrative whole. He laid the groundwork for modern treatment of trauma by understanding the women's symptoms as reality-based and giving them different means of self-expression. When the trauma was set in a coherent narrative, it became integrated and symptoms were alleviated.

Janet was convinced that trauma was a physical as well as an emotional wound, the symptoms of which were manifested in the memory disturbances of his patients. He saw the symptoms as trauma frozen in the body and discovered that these symptoms would abate when the women's stories found another way to be told.

Dr. Janet trusted that what the women held in their bodies was the memory of what had happened to them. He believed that the traumatic wound reached even to the cellular level. Foreshadowing late twentieth-century research, Janet tested the blood and other bodily fluids of those suffering from trauma. He intuitively grasped what research would later demonstrate, that the very biochemistry of those who are traumatized changes. The effects of the wound circulate with the blood of its carrier. The trauma response is robust, chemically expressed, physically experienced, and often very confusing.

Although Pierre Janet's work was picked up by others in the following decades, for a significant period of time the fact that trauma is based in reality became secondary to a concern with intrapsychic processes and conflicts that were seen as the primary causes of symptoms. Much of Janet's work was relegated to the back shelf of science until late in the twentieth century.

A belief in the power of trauma never fully disappeared from psychiatry, however. Pockets of observation and knowledge backed up by clinical experience persisted and created a body of literature that has been validated by our relatively recent ability to image the brain. The violence, displacement, and outright horror of some events in the twentieth century created a global arena for the study of trauma. Much of that history and experience was systematically recorded and studied during and after the Vietnam War. So many people returned from the war with the same symptoms at the same time that significant resources were devoted to trying to understand what was at the root of the suffering.

Post Traumatic Stress Disorder (PTSD) has been defined as an anxiety disorder over the past sixty years. Abram Kadiner, a psychoanalyst and anthropologist, first defined its basic components in 1941 as "Traumatic Neurosis of War." The codification of PTSD brought together many of the previous observations on the effects of trauma, regardless of the battlefield where the violence occurs. The anxiety of PTSD is fed by the inability to keep what happened in the past from intruding into the present. The symptoms cluster in three groups:

- intrusion of the memories

- constriction or numbing of feeling about the trauma

- arousal of the central nervous system.

These symptoms all stem from the normal human response to trauma which becomes problematic if that response cannot be resolved and so continues. They also relate to memory and the difficulty of integrating the powerful affect and physical arousal of the trauma into daily life. The symptoms are the body's way of trying to master the memory, albeit in a disruptive way.

PTSD causes major disruption in all aspects of life, most especially in interpersonal relationships. The symptoms of PTSD are reflective of a continued arousal in response to threat that is perceived by the body as ongoing. Not every person exposed to trauma develops PTSD, though it is frequently spoken of as if it were the only response to trauma. PTSD is an extreme version of symptoms that are experienced by anyone who survives a threatening experience. All people who go through trauma experience some of the symptoms of PTSD. When there is adequate social support and attention to the symptoms, they tend to be resolved more easily.

Taken together and experienced in an extreme way over a period of time, the intrusive, avoidance, and arousal symptoms are criteria for diagnosing Post Traumatic Stress Disorder. Distinctions are made within the diagnostic criteria between single-incident trauma, such as a car accident or a one-time exposure to violence, and ongoing trauma, such as combat or domestic violence. Long-term exposure is likely to result in complex PTSD, an adaptation that becomes part of the personality and its coping mechanisms. PTSD in either form tends to be chronic in that extreme stress, exhaustion, or exposure to similar circumstances will exacerbate the symptoms or cause them to reappear.

The criteria for PTSD diagnosis include a time test: the symptoms must persist for longer than three weeks. By that definition, millions of people in the New York area and around the country qualified for the diagnosis of PTSD by October of 2001. Three weeks was not long enough for the trauma response to be resolved in the body. The trauma response remains active while the fires of the event are still burning—either in reality or in the mind of the survivor. Yet, as was the case after the Oklahoma City bombing, only a small group of people in New York City developed full-blown cases of PTSD after one year.

Most survivors of public traumatic events are able to function at a fairly high level, in part because so much attention is given to processing the trauma. Yet difficulties are common, and the memory continues to impact the present. The wound remains deep, even after people have moved beyond some of their initial responses to the trauma.

The expected symptoms of trauma cluster and linger in a more extreme way in people who have experienced brutal violence, abuse, or threat, in those who are vulnerable because of prior traumatic experiences, such as child abuse, or those who live with a lack of social support or ongoing stress. There is a gender difference in the rate of people who develop full-blown PTSD. The literature indicates that women are more likely to develop PTSD than men; the significance of that observation, however, is not yet completely clear. One of reasons for the seemingly higher incidence of PTSD in women could be rooted in the fact that more women have underlying trauma from previous sexual abuse. The same observation has been made in reference to differing rates for the incidence of depression in the genders. It is possible that the symptoms of both conditions manifest differently in each gender, with aggressivity being more common in males because it is more socially acceptable for them.

Significantly, those whose actions at the time of the trauma were somehow in violation of their personal beliefs suffer most intensely after it. The most intransigent forms of PTSD among Vietnam veterans were among those who were forced to act against conscience by killing people who were noncombatants in the war. The same is true of torture victims who were forced to give information that they believe may have led to the death of others. The inability of a parent to protect a child in situations of domestic abuse can cause the same deepening of distress.

THERE ARE MANY FACTORS THAT NUANCE the recovery process, most especially the severity of the original trauma. What is common to all healing processes is the need to make peace with the memory of what has happened. The sequestered memory needs to be made part of consciousness so that the memory can inform the future rather than foreclosing it. First, however, the physical wounds must be tended with appropriate medical care. Basic human needs such as food, shelter, and clothing must be met. The initial goal of psychological treatment is to stabilize the trauma symptoms through a number of means, including exercise, relaxation training, breathing exercises, and, as needed, medication.

Stabilizing the symptoms of trauma requires a shift in understanding their meaning. The symptoms need to be appreciated as life-preserving resources from a time of extraordinary circumstances. The healing process begins not with trying to push the symptoms away, but rather with trying to understand and befriend them for the great protection they have been. The symptoms originate in human resiliency and are not a sign of weakness or failure. The wound left by trauma can heal only through mobilization of the resources that enabled survival to occur. Stabilization of the symptoms makes it possible to draw on cultural, spiritual, and relational resources to assist in working through traumatic memory so that it can be integrated into the meaning and texture of a life story. That transition requires mercy on oneself for not having acted any differently during the trauma itself, on others for their responses to the distress, and on humanity for the evil capacity that trauma so often reveals. Making peace with memory requires respecting the reactions and processes at work in the face of trauma as in service of life, not proof of hysteria or some type of failure.

Natural Reactions

ONE FRIDAY EVENING WHILE I WAS IN LATIN AMERICA, I went with a group of people to the central plaza. There was a lot of traffic on the narrow streets. It was already dark and drivers were in a hurry to reach their destinations. Walking along the sidewalk, we met three boys who were ten or eleven years old. Just as we reached them, the boys began to fight. One of the smaller boys was pushed into the street. He fell down. I immediately stepped into the street to help him. I extended my hand to him and he grasped it.

Just as he stood up, I saw the headlights of a car approaching us at high speed. I dropped the boy's hand and jumped back onto the sidewalk. The little boy was right behind me. The potentially catastrophic event didn't happen— neither of us was hit by the car. It had worked out well.

Yet, after the fact, I felt guilty about having let go of his hand in the interest of my own survival. I considered it an act of cowardice. Even though the little boy and I both survived, I felt I had betrayed my values in not extending myself automatically for the survival of another. It took years for me to understand the processes that were at work in that situation and to forgive myself for wanting to save my own life.

We all have had the experience of thinking after a very stressful situation "What I should have done or said was . . ." It is physiologically impossible to be stunned, threatened, and intellectually clever at the same time. Because the body's response to threatening situations is initiated and coordinated in the more primitive brain stem, action is taken before the message reaches the frontal lobe of the brain where language forms to describe or process the experience.

Decisions made under threatening circumstances are not rational; they are manifestations of a survival instinct. It is the nature of the physiological response to trauma that what we think of as the rational mind is not the area of the brain aroused to deal with the situation. Much more primary processes take over, and this can cause great confusion and regret later about why we responded to a situation in the way that we did. The engagement of the reptilian brain for survival circumvents the processing of rational information or complex verbal understanding of the situation. The brain is activated to preserve life in the moment; reflection on the experience can occur only later.

Initially, I did not understand that night why all my education, religious formation, and highest ideals seemed to suddenly disappear when I saw the headlights. When I thought about my leap as if it had been a conscious choice, I was deeply disappointed in myself. I had failed my first real test at laying down my life for a friend, and I felt powerful shame. Yet the fact is that it was not a conscious choice but an instinctive reaction, based on a normal and adaptive mechanism. Years later, as I remember the headlights, I know that the moment held a real threat, evoked real fear, and demanded immediate life-preserving action.

While words and rational thought are not the entry point to the brain's response to trauma, they tend to be the first place we turn to try and understand our responses. One of the greatest obstacles to healing from trauma is the feeling that one is somehow culpable for what happened because of a failure to act in a rational, understandable way. Such judgments are usually harsh and far removed from the powerlessness experienced in the moment of trauma. The split second of instinct to save one's life, or the experience of having one's resources overwhelmed by circumstances is neither a crime nor a sin. The feeling that others might have been saved if a different action had been taken, or if one had not acted in the interest of one's own survival, runs counter to the reality that the trauma response is not rational or planned in advance. There is no shame in the truth of being human. Yet re-living the memory of what happened—the emotions that were set aside for the sake of survival, the sense of having somehow failed to be true to one's deeper values—can be the most perplexing and painful part of any healing process.

THE MOST COMMON PSYCHOLOGICAL RESPONSE to a traumatic situation is dissociation. Simple dissociative processes like tuning out of a boring lecture or having no memory of a trip once the destination has been reached are part of daily life. The interstate highway system was deliberately built with some curves to keep drivers from experiencing a trance state called "highway hypnosis." The body is present but the mind is somewhere else. Daydreaming has saved me more than once when I found myself in meetings that I did not want to attend or a conflict situation that I could not resolve. I went for a walk on the beach and did some body surfing instead, all without my body leaving the conference table.

To dissociate from trauma is to separate oneself from the experience, both in the moment of the trauma itself and afterwards. It is an exaggeration of a normal process and response. The statement my husband made in his September 11th phone call—"I feel like I am in a movie"—is a way of creating distance that has an important purpose. It is impossible to grasp the reality and emotional significance of life-threatening events as they are happening. The survival instinct creates a split in consciousness to enable the individual to live through the traumatic event by psychologically removing the self from the situation. It is an out-of-body experience in the sense that a strict differentiation is made between events, feelings, and memory. What is threatening and overwhelming becomes separated from consciousness; the experience is not happening to me. This type of response to trauma is commonly reported, most especially in situations where being conscious of the reality might threaten survival.

Dissociation is the experience of not being present to reality as a way of maintaining an illusion of safety. It is a common form of defense that is taken to an extreme in traumatic situations. The protective feeling of dissociation does not need to continue if the trauma is time-limited, others are aware of the event, and there are good support systems in place. Dissociation is not as readily worked through if the cause of the trauma is hidden or continues over a long period of time. This basically normal response becomes problematic when it separates one from day-to-day reality, or creates a split in consciousness that makes the memory of what happened inaccessible, and so impossible to integrate.

Dissociation is common in situations where abuse occurs at home or where ongoing survival depends on maintaining a relationship with the perpetrator. It is impossible for a child or vulnerable adult to reconcile the violence and violation with economic and emotional dependence on the perpetrator. Abuse perpetrated by a person about whom the victim has positive feelings is more than just a terrible betrayal. The inherent contradiction between Daddy the Monster and Daddy who loves me is too much for a child to bear. It is too threatening and overwhelming to live in the reality of abuse at the hands of someone so close to the victim. Survival depends on splitting off consciousness during the abuse and afterwards. The ongoing nature of domestic abuse virtually requires dissociation. Once physical safety has been achieved—sometimes after years of regular abuse—the physical response continues and the world can be seen as too frightening a place to work through the dissociated material. Establishment of safety is always required as the foundation for healing.

Emotional safety is a major issue for people who have been abused in some way, particularly in childhood. Betrayal of trust early in life due to violence experienced or witnessed creeps into consciousness as a norm; nothing is trustworthy. One of the most destructive effects of trauma is a sense of isolation about and from the story of what happened. It is only when abused women begin to talk to each other that a safe space opens up as a means of escape from the prison of isolation. If resources for expression, social support, and healing are not available, dissociation places the reality of what happened into a separate sphere in human memory. Separation of the memory and its feelings from consciousness or narrative makes it possible to completely forget a traumatic experience or to minimize its emotional and spiritual content.

Dissociated material may well become conscious in bits and pieces, or in physical sensations related to the trauma. The reality of dissociation may become apparent only over time. Partial memory can be more confusing than no memory at all. Dissociation—along with the strange ways in which trauma enters memory—explains the phenomenon of a survivor who "can't get the story straight." Confusion around details or a seeming lack of coherence in narratives of traumatic experience has led to the dismissal of reports of abuse that were later substantiated by external evidence.

Studies of children brought to emergency rooms after verified and documented incidents of sexual abuse have revealed that amnesia or confusion about the story can exist immediately or years later, even in circumstances where the crime was beyond question. Dr. Frank Putnam and his colleagues are conducting a longitudinal study of children who were brought to emergency rooms and treated for physical injuries caused by sexual abuse. Putnam is interested in the long-range effects of sexual abuse and has chosen to study children whose abuse has been documented and is impossible to deny. Twenty years into the study, Putnam has made the interesting finding that many of the children who seemed the least affected by the violations when the incidents occurred had the worst long-term outcomes. Putnam's work demonstrates that the calm, collected victim who is preferred by most of us, may, in fact, be completely dissociated from the experience. Later, the emotion that has been split off comes roaring back in symptoms like depression or rage that are inappropriate for the situation at hand.

At the same time, one of the consistent findings in studies of child abuse is that what makes the difference in whether a child stays dissociated or works through the experience of trauma is the presence of what Dr. Judith Lewis Herman refers to as a "compassionate witness." The witness validates the child's experience and may, at times, be able to step in and change the situation. Even if no intervention is possible, the witness holds the child's reality and prevents isolation.

Unfortunately, many children and others being abused in their homes do not have a compassionate witness to their suffering for many years. Those without a helpful witness suffer a secondary trauma of having nowhere to turn for help. The sense of betrayal is particularly difficult for a child who knew that other adults were aware of the situation and either made no intervention or sent the child back to the abusive situation, having placed on the child's shoulders the responsibility of preventing further abuse: be good and the abuse will stop. The mechanisms of self-protection become a consistent way of being in the world, a way that ensures tremendous suffering and an impoverishment of relationships.

"THE GREAT SORROWS ARE SILENT," runs an Italian proverb. To speak the words of the broken body and spirit is not immediately possible for someone whose survival depends on dissociation. For many, as the trauma is walled off from consciousness, speaking about it at all is difficult, and feels like a repetition of the threat to survival. Whenever silence shrouds traumatic events, the resulting dissociation will exact its own price. The survivors of Hiroshima, the concentration camps, and industrial accidents like the Triangle Shirt Waist Fire, where workers made the now familiar choice to jump rather than burn, told similar stories about the process of trying to go on with life after their experiences. Life was different after the traumatic events, and yet some of the survivors never spoke of the events again. They were terrified into silence. The trauma worked its way through the family system namelessly, and so dissociated from the events that caused the initial fear and pain.

The same kind of secrecy around sexual abuse, drug abuse, suicide, or mental illness in a family can keep memory and healing at bay. The secrets may well be linked; substance abuse in response to trauma is common. That the next generation is affected by the addiction is an extension of the original traumatic wound. Secrets have a way of clustering together in an attempt to protect the self. The pain of a grandparent's hidden suicide finds its way into subsequent generations, largely with the sense of confusion that accompanies a deep pain that remains unnamed.

More insidiously, further damage is done by the press of the trauma trapped within the body. Memory that is contained so carefully and split from awareness can become threatening when it breaks through the barrier to consciousness. It is terrifying to come into the presence of feelings and memory pieces that were previously unknown. The possibility of their integration initially feels like an impossible hope, let alone material for the process of transformation.

Dissociation occurs on the social and cultural level as well as in the lives of individuals. Robert J. Lifton described this response on a societal level as psychic numbing—the tuning out of what is unbearable to remember. His observations were based on interviews with people in Hiroshima and Nagasaki who had survived the nuclear bombs. He noted a general lack of emotion in describing the initial destruction of the attack and the subsequent loss of life from radiation-induced diseases. Echoing the observations of others, he suggested that the numbing of emotions served the purpose of survival in the short term. The long-term danger lies in the fact that individuals who cannot process their pain suffer greatly and humanity as a whole is deprived of the opportunity of learning the actual consequences of actions. Horrors too powerful to be claimed are set aside in a kind of protective act. Lifton observed that the nuclear proliferation of the cold war was a classic case of psychic numbing. How could we otherwise live next to nuclear power plants or silos and not be paralyzed with fear? But how could we hope for peace without confronting the horror? How can a narrative and its lessons be coaxed out of hiding when silence has been the basis for survival?

It seems that dissociated pain and its consequences can begin to enter consciousness only when we choose to reenact Freud's dilemma in a way that does not require that knowledge be split in two. When beliefs about self or culture are threatened by the evidence of one's own experience, we may simply have to name and suffer the contradictions of what we would bury and what we long to bring into the light. Dissociation isolates the trauma and its feelings within the person and, on a larger scale, within society. It begins to heal only when there is a meaningful connection with another human being who has the capacity to believe the story and dares to admit, "Me, too."

The isolation of trauma has touched us all. Recognition of its reality begins the transformation of memory from an intrusive threat to a source of strength. The greatest power of memory that is claimed lies in its ability to nurture imagination of a different future. Memory is the repository of hope; we know that life is possible in the future when we recognize its tenacity in the past.

We are inclined to think of memory as a primarily verbal process. Yet to fully receive the memory of trauma, we must be willing to challenge our assumptions about how stories are remembered and retold. The verbal narrative is rarely the first and certainly not the only step in the process.

Living Memory

TRAUMA LITERATURE DIFFERENTIATES BETWEEN THE human reaction to natural disaster and the human reaction to suffering caused by other human beings. The understanding is that the intentionality of human actions makes them more difficult to comprehend. Yet increasingly the distinction blurs as it becomes known that patterns of weather and movement of the earth's surface are affected by human actions. The earth itself is traumatized, suffering an interruption in the circle of creation, and all living creatures, including human beings, are wounded.

The earth's wound is a memory that is revealed when mudslides resulting from irresponsible forestry wipe away the shacks of the poor. Poisonous PCBs in Hudson River mud find their way into fish that are eaten by pregnant women. The Passaic River in New Jersey—the state with the highest cancer rate in the nation—carries the molecular remnants of the chemical Agent Orange that was manufactured along its banks. A substance created to destroy the foliage in Vietnam made its way around the world only to return suffering to its place of origin through the cells of those exposed to the toxins. What killed the trees also kills the people.

The diversion of water for irrigation in Central Asia has led to the destruction of the Aral Sea, perhaps the worst ecological disaster created by human beings. The draining of more than 75 percent of the water in the sea has left the seabed exposed. The toxic salt and dust have traveled on the wind and destroyed the fertile Amu Darya delta. Drinking water contaminated by pesticides and other chemicals has led to very high infant mortality, cancer, and other diseases. The earth trauma caused by destruction of the sea and its delta returns to humans in a circle of trauma that runs counter to the circle of life. Sometimes earth trauma is as invisible to the naked eye as the sequestered trauma of human beings. Yet the earth holds the memories of her trauma and teaches us powerful lessons about our own.

The fertile and seemingly endless expanse of fields in Iowa creates a peaceful vision of a hospitable land. Each summer the growing crops extend to a horizon as limitless as the sea that once occupied the space, a sea that sometimes yields its remnants in fossils found by a farmer's plow. Beneath the fertile soil, the shale records the memory of a time and its upheavals that are now hidden from view. That memory reminds us that the living processes of the earth are not to be claimed as something under human control. The mammoth rocks and the rich black topsoil tell the story of how earth has changed over the centuries. The earth remembers with clarity changes that were forced against the natural order.

The extraordinarily productive land is forced into even greater yields by the creation of large fields whose trees have been removed, naked fields in winter that have no unharvested roots to serve as anchors for the soil. The land and rivers of the Midwestern United States are examples of nature being managed in a way that increases productivity while tampering with earth's original design. Each spring the muddy waters of local streams and mighty rivers run black with the fertile soil that slips away from the land where it belongs because productivity has become more important than conservation.

As the land was being made more productive, the rivers were being tamed. The Mississippi was once a wild river. It sometimes changed channels so abruptly from one season to the next that, during the westward expansion, explorers sometimes returned to a spot chosen the previous year as the site for a town only to discover that the river was not where they had left it. The wandering channels created miles of backwater that absorbed the deluge of spring's melted snow and were part of the river's living ecosystem. The river's unpredictability made it difficult for steamboat captains to navigate up the channel. That the deep spaces and shallow rocks were changeable made the river an untrustworthy place to travel, even as its length connected north and south in a continuous flow, right through the middle of the continent.

Being able to pass safely through the river was an economic necessity. The overflow into backwater areas created its own difficulties, not the least of which was the impossibility of planting in or living on the fertile flood plain. It was also hard to identify the lines of private property when the river was free to change the spaces to which one claimed a title. All these were intolerable and life-threatening problems in a growing country that wanted every square inch of tillable soil and needed a dependable means of bringing the bountiful harvest to market.

Over the course of fifty years, a massive civil engineering project forced the Mississippi and its tributaries into more predictable, passable channels. The intricacy and scope of the project were unparalleled in history of civil engineering.

Locks and dams, levees and spillways managed the river in ways that were a technological marvel. There was little recognition at the time when the project was being carried out that there is an inherent contradiction in trying to increase the earth's productivity while changing the course of one of her major rivers.

Control seemed to be in the service of survival. A long, vital river was contained with an expectation of permanence, stability, and a clear demarcation between land and water. The tributary system of the Mississippi, which stretches its veins across the Midwest, was affected by the straightening of the river toward which its water flowed. The tributaries were poised to received overflow water from the Mississippi, and vice versa. The space to hold the waters was compromised.

The complicated engineering system worked, however, and most of the time the wild river was tamed. Yet the river remembered its channels. Standing on bluffs above the Mississippi, it is possible to see remnants of channel changes, the islands, trees, and little lakes existing as orphans a mile or more away from the main channel. In spite of human attempts at control, the river knew where it wanted to go and, with enough water, it could again be more powerful than the hardest stone of a wing dam or the most clever system of containment.

When in 1993 there came a season of unprecedented rains, the tender shoots of early planting were carried into rivers that soon turned muddy and overflowed. The mighty river and her tributaries could not be stopped by flood control projects or human will. All of the natural places, the flood plains where the constant rains could overflow, had been claimed as dependable land. The river had been bent out of shape, and in reasserting itself it was an angry force. The slightest wind uprooted the trees from the gelatinous soil. A satellite photo showed flood water backed up into the tributaries to create an expanse of water the size of Lake Superior. In the place of endless crops planted on a dry seabed, that year the land become an island in the midst of an endless bay.

The drama on the human level was compelling. Evacuated from their homes, hundreds of people watched more rain fall as they looked out the windows of gymnasiums, church basements, and other spaces where they had fled for safety in their powerlessness. People lost their homes, their land, and the possessions that carried family memory. There were desperate acts. One man tried to save his home by breaking the levee on the opposite side of the river in an effort to direct the flow of the river into someone else's state. Even the dead were disturbed as rushing water opened graves and sent long-buried bodies on an unexpected and horrifying journey downstream. A series of storms led to a middle-of-the-night rupture of a dam on the Iowa River. A furious wall of water washed away a road and several feet of topsoil beneath it.

When the waters receded in that area, a great surprise was discovered. The tons of earth moved by the flood revealed a huge, previously unknown deposit of prehistoric fossils, one of the largest such deposits ever found. Even more amazing was the way it was revealed. While the flood had destroyed the familiar landscape and its markers of meaning and memory, it had exposed a deeper, more original memory, that of the ancient seabeds. The wonder of these layers of memory existing unknown beneath our feet helped to sustain people after the devastation of the flood. Geologists and students came from all over the country to see the newly exposed memory of the earth. The site drew pilgrimages of photographers and families with babies in backpacks and older children fascinated by the rocks. As people looked at the fossils, they spontaneously told each other their stories of the flood. Individual stories were placed into a narrative of common memory. The flood divided the memory of land into a before and after time; the fossils held the deep memory that mysteriously bridged those eras and restored a sense of meaning and wonder.

The following summer, barges moved carefully up the river, their pilots aware that the channel was changed and filled with submerged and unknown artifacts of the flood. The water that had caused destruction the previous year led to a stunningly beautiful growing season with vibrant prairie flowers and a plentiful harvest. Those fields that were plowed deeply after the flood became part of a mysterious rebirth. The rebuilding after the flood was done with new respect and appreciation for the power of unclaimed memory.

RECOLLECTION OF TRAUMA often feels like a terrible flood that has the power to destroy life. The containment of the memory—like the straightening of a mighty river, is ironic in that the energy of the memory is always with us, more powerful and potentially destructive precisely because of our attempts to manage its reality. The remembering earth holds the stories and the knowledge of where the water was meant to flow.

We are of the earth. We carry her elements in our bodies—copper, iron, magnesium, and salts, to name a few—and if those elements are disturbed, health is affected. We carry the memory of trauma in our bodies, the layers on its crust shaped and changed by processes beneath the surface, the core of fire. Each element of our being is connected to an earth that responds and remembers.

The concept that memory exists only in the brain fails to appreciate the complexity of the human body. The cells of our immune system remember whether or not they have been exposed to a particular infectious agent. Our musculature holds the memory of learning to walk and talk. Memory exists in the totality of our being. Our spirit is strengthened in the revelation of deep mysteries held by our remembering bodies. The original channels of life exist within us, available when the need for constriction has passed. The courage of remembering can lead us to discover the deep seabed traces of what has always been. What floods the body and soul also reveals the deeper memory of our humanity. The memory of life emerging from death like vibrant prairie flowers can sustain the most flooded heart, even if the initial impression of hope is as skeletal as the markings of ancient marine life found a thousand miles from any known sea.

Tending to memory is a physical, spiritual, and emotional process. Without memory, we cannot know who we are. Memory is a matter of the soul. Individuals who are experiencing trauma learn from others who have survived similar experiences. The ability to stand in the truth of what has happened in life holds the power of transformation; memory that is linked to compassion births forgiveness of oneself for the limitations of being human and a deep understanding of the pain of others. Memory that is cared for as a sacred part of the human story becomes the basis for hope and a hospitality of heart large enough to accept the sorrows of what cannot be changed.

A century ago, Dr. Pierre Janet observed, and subsequent science has documented, that there is a qualitative difference between how ordinary events of life are remembered and retold and the narratives and memory of trauma. Janet noted that normal memory is the action of telling oneself or another the story of experiences. It is sequential and expressed in its proper tense. Past is separated from present in the process of what Janet called "ordinary memory."

The memory of trauma, however, is not in the past. It is present and re-experienced with the intensity of the original events. There is no time sequence—the memory simply is without the perspective of sequence and understanding. A mixed and confusing jumble of sensory and bodily experiences—hearing sounds, smelling something, seeing images of the trauma, feeling hands tremble and heart race as if the body is currently under attack—are the hallmarks of traumatic memory. There is a frozen aspect to the narratives of trauma, as though the experience lives in a separate place within the individual. The trauma continues as a living event. It is spoken of as if the events are still happening or are in the very recent past, regardless of how many years have gone by since the events actually happened There is an immediacy about traumatic memory. A study of women who had lost children of any age revealed that, no matter how many years had passed since the death or how much healing had occurred, the women's narratives were constructed as if the death had just happened.

Shifting from that sense of immediacy to the creation of a memorial sense of events is never really complete, even as the distress caused by the trauma is ameliorated. The bodies of trauma survivors indeed hold their stories. This became quite clear when sophisticated scans and other types of laboratory advances made it possible to "look inside" the brain and learn more about how it functions. While we have only begun to learn about the mysterious powers of the brain, what we know so far documents in a visual way the processes long described by victims of trauma and the people around them. Dr. Janet's work has found validation in modern science and in the growing articulation of human experience.

That the nature of traumatic memory is different is likely due to a number of factors. Traumatic memory is distinct because overwhelming events are responded to by the primitive parts of the brain, which then alert the whole body to go into action. The imprint of the event is made in the lower brain under circumstances in which the level of stress hormones is very high. The nature of the memory is not verbal because it is imprinted before reaching the frontal lobe of the brain.

We have both implicit and explicit memory systems in our bodies. The implicit memory holds the knowledge of how to ride a bike, play a game, or do a dance. More important, it lets the body remember how to perform the fundamental yet involuntary acts of living such as breathing and, at times, mobilizing in the face of a threat. Explicit memory holds acquired knowledge and experience. It also preserves the memory that is narrative—past experience organized through language.

Trauma enters the body through the mechanisms of the implicit memory. The aftermath of trauma's impact is stored in the tissues of the body: the tense muscles, the quickly beating heart, the holding of the breath. These physical reminders of trauma can become the focus of awareness without any connection being made between the physical pain and the trauma.

WHAT CANNOT BE GIVEN VOICE cannot be integrated and healed. It requires tremendous psychic and societal energy to keep the wound of trauma away from consciousness. When what seems too much to bear becomes inaccessible, the memory presents itself in startling and disturbing ways. Intrusive memories bring the experience and all of the accompanying feelings to consciousness vividly and without permission. The images that intrude are representative of sights or experiences that we may have generally hidden or made a Herculean effort not to think about.

Early one morning I was on my way to LaGuardia Airport in New York. The taxi driver was forced to stop on the Triboro Bridge because of police activity. We were among the first to arrive on this scene. As I was wondering about whether or not I would miss my plane, I glanced out the window. Less than ten feet away from me was the dead body of a young man. I could see his face, his shoes, his jacket pockets. The body did not have an obvious fatal injury, but it seemed unlikely that the man had died of natural causes.

Unlike in many countries of the world, bodies along the side of the road are not part of common experience in the United States. After I had taken in the scene, I turned to a book until we were allowed to drive again. I reached the airport, went through the security gates, and was waiting quietly for my plane when the clear image of the body popped into my mind. This continued for the next few days. The image of the young man dead on the bridge intruded upon my consciousness and demanded attention. The more that I tried to forget the sight, the more present it became to me.

Eventually, I talked with a friend about it and the images faded. This was a limited, self-contained trauma, but its memory was intruding on me until I gave it some respect and tended to its power. The memories of more complicated trauma can be much more troublesome and difficult to endure.

The intrusion of traumatic memories is understandably upsetting. Such memories seemingly come unbidden and unrelated to current thoughts or circumstances. At a happy event, images from a recent death intrude. While listening to someone else, concentration is interrupted by an intense memory and images that are difficult to dismiss. There is an awareness that this is a memory of something in the past, yet it is hard to dismiss or integrate the memory. Intrusive memories are like a fragment of a song that plays again and again, the annoying tune that you cannot get out of your head until its distraction has run its course. These memories, however, are much more disturbing.

It is confusing to experience intrusive memories because of the lack of connection between the material in the memory and when and how it appears. The memory takes hold without its context, like the recollection of a past loss mysteriously pressing into consciousness during a pleasant meal. The image barges in without permission and is resistant to being set aside; powerlessness over the memory then becomes a stressor of its own.

Though intrusive memories themselves can resemble the passing frames of a movie, what is playing on the invisible screen is real and personal. It is the picture of the car approaching in slow motion, the sound of the crash, the helplessness of being injured. It is the sight of a loved one in a coffin, a conflictive conversation, violence experienced or witnessed. Intrusive memories tend to be an intense representation of the cause of the wound, whatever that cause might be.

Unlike intrusive memories, which carry some understanding that what is coming to mind is a past event, people experiencing flashbacks are temporarily living in the moment of the trauma with all the attending physical anguish. Flashbacks are a momentary loss of contact with current reality because of a memory so vivid that it is alive in the moment. Most people experience consciousness shifts so complete that there is a confusion of time and space. Many of these types of flashbacks occur and pass from our minds without causing distress. When I hear Spanish spoken on the subway, for example, there is always a split second when I am back in Bolivia learning the language. It jars me when the subway stops and I find myself in New York. Vivid as it may be, that type of flashback is not entirely unpleasant.

The flashbacks of trauma survivors, however, evoke the original sense of terror and helplessness. Flashbacks are a function of memory presented in such a way that the material of the past is the agony of the present. Flashbacks have been dramatically represented in the actions of people who have hurt others in the belief that they are back in the situation of trauma. The people being screamed at are not neighbors, for example; they are enemy soldiers. More common is a disruption of consciousness that is fleeting, but extremely powerful and disorienting.

Both flashbacks and intrusive memories are the reality of the wound breaking through consciousness. It has been suggested that part of the reason intrusive symptoms present as they do stems from the fact that memories of events that happen in moments of extreme stress must work their way from implicit to explicit memory.

Intrusive symptoms are part of a process that seeks to restore equilibrium by bringing dissociated material to consciousness. The disruptive symptoms are a signal that the traumatic material is in need of attention. Unfortunately, by the time the disruption occurs, there may have been a passage of time or strong dissociation that obscured the connection between the symptom and the original traumatic event; this can be, at best, extremely confusing. The frequently asked question, "Why can't I stop thinking about this after all this time?" testifies to the durability of memory powerful enough to create the urgency of intrusive symptoms.

There is a special type of anxiety that arises from the feeling that control over thoughts, memory, and cognition has been lost. The power of intrusive symptoms can lead people to believe that they are going crazy, or, more threatening still, will go crazy if they pay attention to the disorienting symptoms. Recognition of the simple reality that intrusive memories, no matter how distressing, are part of a normal process of working through trauma can go a long way toward easing the anxiety about loss of control.

When under threat, the body becomes vigilant and acutely aware of incoming messages and stressors. The heightening of senses that aids in escape from perceived danger becomes problematic if it continues in daily life. The body is aware of possible dangers in all circumstances. One can experience the hyper-alert, hyper-vigilant state even in situations that seem objectively safe. Every noise or touch elicits the startle response. People having such an experience constantly scan their surroundings for danger and escape routes, both physical and emotional. They are attuned to noises and possibilities that others take for granted; each wail of a rescue engine sounds different to a person who has experienced a fire.

SHORTLY AFTER THE SEPTEMBER 11TH ATTACKS, I was on a flight into New York that circled the city for over an hour. The pilot said that we were not landing because lightning was striking close to the ground. We circled so long that the plane ran out of fuel. Rather than landing at LaGuardia Airport, we landed at Kennedy. Passengers were given a choice of departing the plane there or waiting for refueling and then taking a very brief flight to LaGuardia. When those options were presented, the level of anxiety in the cabin rose perceptibly. Many of the travelers were convinced that something sinister was at work, that there had to be a threat of some kind that had kept the plane from landing at LaGuardia. I had the same thoughts. Something must have happened again in New York City and the truth was being withheld to prevent panic.

Most of the passengers left the plane when it landed at Kennedy Airport, and the only reason that I didn't was that I was too tired to move. Not for the first time in my life, exhaustion trumped fear. Refueled, the plane took off and landed so quickly that it felt like one smooth action. The only threat really had been lightning, but given the heightened state of people's nerves after 9/11, such an explanation seemed impossible.

Hyper-vigilance leads to physical exhaustion and at the same time, inhibits restful sleep. How can a person surrender to sleep when it is necessary to constantly be on the alert for danger? Difficulty falling asleep and staying asleep, awakening abruptly with a pounding heart and constricted breathing in the middle of the night, and hypersensitivity to noise are all common. Nightmares about the actual traumatic experience or some symbolic representation of that experience cause distress and further damage the ability to sleep. To close one's eyes is to risk the intrusion of memories and the reawakening of terror.

I did not fall sleep for two days after undergoing major surgery under an epidermal anesthesia that failed. I felt much more than I should have during the surgery. It was an excruciating and terrifying experience, compounded by the surgeon's complaint that I was being uncooperative. When the surgery was over and morphine was running through my veins, I could not afford to sleep lest there be a further assault on my body. To the amazement of the nurses, I remained wide awake. Every time I tried to close my eyes, I was back in the utter helplessness of the operating room. The anesthesiologist stopped by my room to apologize and recommended that I never have that particular type of block again. I have had three subsequent surgeries and there have been no problems with the anesthesia. Yet each time, my last conscious thought has been, "I hope to God that this works," and after each surgery sleep eluded me until I felt the safety of my own bed. The vigilance has remained as a powerful warning: this promise of painless surgery cannot be trusted.

Trauma changes one's perception of the world. The loss of safety means the first thing noticed and assessed in any situation is potential harm or injury. This exhausting process can go on without conscious awareness and often forecloses interventions or solutions that could be positive and healing. The impact on interpersonal relationships is profound; hypervigilant people will jump when touched. The perceived lack of everyday safety and the constant vigilance make the vulnerability required in intimate relationships too terrifying to tolerate. Trauma violates a sense of trust in how the world works, how other people behave, and what kind of protection can be expected from God. The instinct to run for one's life is transferred from the original situation to constant emotional response of avoidance. Anything that will bring one back in touch with the experience of the trauma is a threat and therefore to be avoided.

My father was a veteran of World War II. He was trained as a pilot and navigator and it was his responsibility to determine when the plane was directly over the bombing target. Because the plane flew in such dangerous conditions, there was a high rate of mortality among these pilots. The death of colleagues and friends was a daily reality for people who knew that they were flying under the same risks as the people who had died.

My father once told me that he felt physically ill when he saw pictures of the destruction caused by the bombs. After his death, I read his flight logbook. Among other things, the log described a potentially deadly plane crash that he survived. His entry ended with the words "I don't think I want to fly any more." Two days later, he was back in the air, even though his neck had been permanently injured in the crash. For the rest of his life, though he was often in airplanes, my father could not stand the smell of lamb cooking. It took him back to England and the meals he ate before going on the bombing runs over Germany, all of them undertaken in the shadow of death. His avoidance of mutton was one of the lesser symptoms of his trauma from the war, but it spoke volumes about how much the experience of trauma seeps into daily life.

Trauma survivors perceive acknowledgment of the reality and its accompanying feelings as threatening to whatever adaptations they have made. Thus, all reminders become enemies that must be kept at bay. Avoidance becomes symptomatic when the need to stay away from emotions or memories related to trauma becomes a limitation in life or leads to behavior that is destructive. Numbing of feelings with drugs, alcohol, food, or other substances creates difficulty because such behavior can lead to addiction. Pleasure is sacrificed if it awakens memory of the trauma. This is particularly a problem for people who have survived sexual assault. The deepest of physical pleasures is linked with horrible pain that comes to eclipse desire. Pleasure of any kind is avoided because the experience of emotion can activate memories of the abuse. Learning to differentiate past from present is a difficult undertaking when the wound is so sensitive. Better, it would seem, to avoid intimacy altogether.

Much suffering can be put under wraps by emotional indifference or detachment. The accompanying language of "it's no big deal" speaks most to the desire that the trauma not be revisited in any way. Avoidance of people, places, or things that might "bring back the memories" can erode the support system that is needed for healing. Trauma survivors may avoid friends who are somehow connected to a deceased loved one because of the reminder not just of happy times but also of the rupture of the loss. Withdrawal from other people who have experienced the same type of pain or loss, or who seem to be graced with the very things that are no longer available to the traumatized person, is common. The woman who has lost a baby cannot bear to see other women's babies, so she may avoid circumstances where there will be children.

That avoidance is impossible, however, because as any woman who has had a miscarriage or buried a child can tell you, the trauma focuses sight in such a way that the little ones are all she can see in the world. What has been personally lost seems to be present everywhere. It is difficult for the millions of people who have been affected by violence to live in a society where everyday language is laced with references to killing or destruction. To avoid the mention or experience of violence is virtually impossible, even if one deeply withdraws from others.

The body and heart become constricted when avoidance of pain is a primary motivator. It is hoped that by feeling nothing, the pain of the trauma will be avoided. Life is narrowed by this constriction, and, as a result, healing cannot take place in the body. This type of constriction easily becomes habitual, and there is often no awareness of the loss it causes.

The cost of constriction in the body recently came home to me in a surprising way. When first diagnosed with a chronic arthritic disease, I went from feeling young and healthy to living with the encroaching fear that I am fragile, that my bones may not be strong enough to support me. I was literally afraid of breaking. As the disease worsened, I became wary of any activity that I thought might cause more pain. I learned that, to be mobile, I had to press the edges of that fear. At the same time, I had to learn a difficult lesson about balance and limits. It is an incomplete lesson that often must teach me anew the strength and limitations of my body. I face the challenge every day. Along the way, I gave up dancing. I narrowed my options, choosing a pathway through life that would not include the joy of the dance for fear of the pain it would cause. Still, I knew that I needed to test that constriction with the strengthening, healing effect of movement.

Yet pain is a fearsome thing and, over time, it can gradually distort the sense of possibility. About the time that I had decided I would live the rest of my life without attempting to dance, my husband and I went to a wedding. A particularly good band playing at the reception roused in me the need to tap my toes and move my body. My husband and I ended up dancing to several songs, including the twist. The dancing did lead to a bit more pain the next day, but it was worth the engagement with life and the sense of well-being that came from knowing I could move my body without fear. I learned that not all dancing needs to be avoided, even though all-night marathons are out of the question for me. My previous rigid constriction had taken away an important part of my capacity for joy.

People who have constricted themselves to protect against the feelings of their own injury cannot risk participating in the dance of their emotional life. As with other attempts to control the flow of feelings associated with trauma, it takes a great deal of effort to maintain the constriction. The effort becomes self-reinforcing over time as the fear of pain begins to erase the possibility of taking any chances and what was once a temporary defense becomes an impoverished way of life.

Like the other clusters of symptoms, constriction undermines interpersonal relationships and reinforces the sense of isolation that is inherently part of traumatic experience. If terror, loss, or grief result in constriction, the possibility for soothing love and joy is also narrowed. Interpersonal relationships become dangerous territory because the awakening of any feeling leads to fear of experiencing the feelings related to the trauma. All feeling, and thus all movement, must be guarded against and avoided.

A seemingly opposite reaction to trauma is to seek to resolve it by taking risks that in some way reenact the traumatic event. Someone who has survived a terrible car accident may become a reckless driver, or a survivor of an assault may be drawn to dangerous situations where a subsequent attack is possible. Risk-taking behavior can also be quite subtle, a pushing of limits that brings one to the edge of danger. Excessive activity undertaken to dull the trauma can press the confines of safety while at the same time bringing social reward. "I don't know how he does it" is perhaps better framed as "I don't know why he does it." People who work in human services and are affected by the trauma of others are tempted to overextend themselves through endless activity. Ostensibly, the reason for such over-activity may be the desire to help more people. It may also be a way of avoiding the feelings provoked in the caregiver by witnessing the suffering of others.

ALTHOUGH THERE ARE CIRCUMSTANCES that are traumatic to anyone, there are no objective ways of predetermining how a particular event will affect an individual. The variables of previous life experience, age, sensitivity, and other complicating factors or vulnerabilities in life such as illness or unresolved loss all influence how a traumatic event will be experienced by a particular individual. Some people can become deeply disturbed or traumatized by events that others might find insignificant. To one person, the sight of a snake in the woods might be a reasonable and predictable aspect of experiencing nature. To another it might be a reminder of a terrifying previous experience with a snake. A twelve-year-old child who is temporarily separated from her mother in a store will have a very different experience than a three-year-old child in the same circumstances.

Because we never fully know the inner life of another person, it is important not to judge the intensity of an individual's reaction to an event. It is equally important to trust our own reactions and experiences. The things that startle and haunt us cannot be minimized, and for many of us, they are not the same. Likewise, the timetable for resolution of trauma is highly individualized.

One of the determining factors in how trauma will affect an adult is the strength of the person's resources to deal with the experience of helplessness. Single-incident trauma can be reacted to in different ways by adults, depending on life history and personal beliefs about one's sense of agency in life and commitment to growth. Those who experience a traumatic event and have already established support systems and healthy habits will recover more quickly than people who lack such resources. If a person's experience of trauma is linked to previous unresolved trauma, the wound is much deeper and healing is more complex.

Trauma in childhood interrupts the natural flow of development that initiates and strengthens the very resources required to face future threats in an intact way. Some type of accommodation has to be made in childhood trauma and the same types of coping mechanisms may be brought to bear in subsequent experience. A traumatized child will have great difficulty establishing a sense of agency or personal empowerment in life. The elements most needed in dealing with trauma—including establishing a support system, retaining hope for the future, and practicing healthy habits—are the ones most impacted by childhood trauma. It is important to withhold judgment of oneself or others in the face of trauma; the uniqueness of each life story holds the best promises for healing.

Trauma and the power of healing are intrinsically part of the human and divine story. Both the wound and its healing can be visualized on the cellular level with sophisticated brain scans. Ways of alleviating trauma symptoms are as ancient as the original descriptions. Religious healing rituals can include both sacramental and non-sacramental expression. A common practice in ancient healing rituals around the world involves returning to the site where something awful has happened and reclaiming it as a friendly part of the earth. The Aymara, an indigenous people of the Andes, perform a ritual with incense and prayer that recognizes the scar of what has happened and reclaims the spirit of both the earth and the victims of tragedy. At the scene of an automobile accident, for example, the Aymara will place on the ground clothing from the people involved in the accident. The offering of prayers and the rising of the incense around the clothing are means of honoring the loss and restoring the balance of the earth. The cosmology that embraces the ceremony is a profound relationship with the earth mother (Pachemama) and the spirit world that inhabits our dreams and visions. Bringing these elements together ceremoniously is a deeply healing process.

Trauma has been expressed and mended through literature, art, music, and spirituality throughout human history. Entire creative forms have given voice and a new shape to traumatic experience. A particularly American example of this is the blues and gospel music that tell stories of oppression with beautiful notes and rhythms. Artistic and spiritual expressions of trauma are linked to observable healing processes in the human body. The calming effects of music register in visible shifts in brain scans of the listener. Observable changes in vital signs reflect the capacity of the arts to both calm the symptoms of trauma and give pathways of expression to the traumatized. These resources for working through trauma have been used over centuries and in situations where individual psychotherapy was not within the realm of imagination. But singing and dancing, praying and weeping are always close at hand.

The claiming of dissociated memory, the restoration of social connections, and the creation of reliable areas of safety are all part of the healing process and become its first fruits. Nothing can change the reality of what has happened, but the acute symptoms can be relieved and a new appropriation of meaning can be made. How much time is required for healing from the acute symptoms of trauma depends upon the renewal of interpersonal relationships, reduction of physical symptoms, and a sense of mastery over memories of the injury. The wound may be a scar that is capable of being reopened, but the reality of the suffering becomes part of the human story that informs us for the rest of our lives. There may always be tenderness, but the rawness of the wound does yield to regeneration. First, however, the survivor must take ownership of its reality.

People heal from trauma when they find a way to hold the historic memory of their suffering. Sometimes survival depends on silence, and it is only in the transition to relative safety that the stories can begin to be told. For children who have suffered abuse, this often is not possible until adulthood. Unfortunately, after years of internally managing trauma, sometimes through potentially damaging behavior, the cause may have long been dissociated from the effect.

There can be immense pressure exerted in families and societies to keep quiet about individual trauma or not to recognize violence against others for what it is. Families can be constructed around a terrified silence about wounds suffered by the powerless. Breaking the silence around the memory of abuse can be so dangerous and interpersonally threatening that a survivor of domestic violence usually needs to reach outside the immediate family circle for assistance in understanding the meaning and power of the memory. Therapists, support groups, artistic expression, and spirituality are all resources for the individual, as well as group, healing of memory.

Like the healing of the earth, human healing is a gradual, living process. It takes time for uprooted trees to trust the soil enough to sink new roots and reach for the light. Many of the most distressing elements of the traumatic wound are based on the need to keep memory of the trauma out of consciousness. Befriending the memory by claiming its reality is a significant step in the alleviation of symptoms and the making of meaning. Trauma creates a new appreciation of the flood plain, that fertile ground that needs to be respected, a middle ground where the flood of feelings and memories can advance and recede without destroying life. The memory of the earth and the body can be honored in that fertile place. Yet finding a middle ground can be a difficult process. The desire to keep the trauma contained and at bay by building right up to its edges with the hope of containment, or running so fast that feelings can't catch up, is powerful and seductive. It may work for a while, but memory that is not paid honor will find other ways to make its presence known. Another temptation is the desire to hold onto the trauma because it feels secure or because it seems like a betrayal of one's own experience to lessen the pain of the trauma.

In either case, there comes a time for a conscious choice about the way in which the process of memory will be regarded. Fundamental respect for memory is a liberating choice because it begins the process of differentiating then from now, the dead from the living. It is the decision to believe that there is more to us than the trauma itself; it is the gateway to hope for the future. The revisiting of the memory can be expressed in many forms, as evidenced by the diverse ways in which emotion finds expression. The understanding of past events will be revisited and adjusted in the course of the life cycle.

The memory of trauma is never neutral. Meanings attached to memories reveal their true nature. These are the memories around which life significantly changed. This is a key component in transformation of the trauma because it is possible for the telling of the story to become an end in itself. If the claiming of memory and the telling of the story do not lead to a movement toward other people, it will fuel bitterness instead of facilitating healing. The importance of personal and communal memory is its ability to shape the present and the future. The choice to allow the memory to lead to new possibilities is a conscious one. Memory has been called upon in human history often as a justification for actions that lead to a rupture in relationships. This happens on the personal, interpersonal, and communal levels. Many a war has been fought in the name of honoring a memory; many an interpersonal relationship has been torn apart by the inability to bear the reality of past events.

Memory that leads back into bitterness and violence is itself damaging because it is impossible to grow beyond the power of the events themselves. There is always a reason to look for someone to blame and to try and exact revenge in the face of the inexplicable. Much more is required for compassion to be born. It is a holding of the truth in a self-forgiving way. Nothing can change what has happened or the actions taken in response to traumatic events. The memory is just that—recollection, not ongoing fact. The walls that separated the memory from consciousness can be transformed into living, breathing bearers of the story. Memory that is properly recognized can become a source of life.

The choice to honor memory as it is—not as a sign of failure or hatred of self or others—makes the memory itself a conduit for meaning. The memory of being slaves in Egypt is converted within the hospitality code into a source of empathy, the fossils revealed by the waters of a sorrowful flood. The process of honoring the memory of trauma is nothing less than letting the river of life flow again.

Waters of Grief

Generations born after the first satellite photos of the delicate blue earth have difficulty grasping that for most of human history, we did not know what our planet looked like from space. Though we had long known that three-fourths of the earth's surface is water, the photos showed the beauty and the intricacy of oceans, seas, rivers, and land masses. There had never been a picture of the planet from that perspective. The absence of borders and boundaries over which people had fought wars, the unity of the waters, and the interconnectedness of all elements of the earth had never been seen so clearly.

The photo demanded that we expand our sight and definition of what the Anglican Book of Common Prayer calls "earth, our island home." The imagery of Genesis, in which God begins creation with the separation of the waters, takes on new meaning when visualized so explicitly. What had been unknown suddenly became known, and we could never think of earth—or heaven—in the same way.

Water gives buoyancy to our cells. It is the elemental substance in our eyes, brains, blood, and organs. We die quickly when deprived of water. I understood that reality in a new way when a dehydrating virus left me in need of IV fluids. There was a moment when the flow of liquids into my veins transformed me from a state of confusion and dizziness to a crystal-clear sense of being alive again. I understood then in my body that vitality is dependent on water.

The water cycle within the body as well as on the earth requires continuous movement, a balance of rain and evaporation, and storage of moisture in settings as diverse—and as intricately linked—as ground water and our own skin. Only a small portion of the waters of earth can be consumed by humans and two-thirds of that supply is frozen in glaciers and snow caps. We may drink today from aquifers whose water fell as rain during the lifetime of Jesus Christ. What works its way into our food may be the water of this season's rains. Water from one side of the earth moves across the planet and, when we meet it, the water feels brand new.

The sources of water are sometimes far away and difficult to tap, especially in situations where the population exceeds the potential of the land to sustain it. For that reason, access to water is rapidly becoming a pressing global issue. The delicate element that has the capacity to carve through stone can be turned into a carrier of death.

The trauma of thirst and the struggle for water rights is ancient. Biblical references to water are informed by the fact that, while the rainfall of Israel was sufficient to support agriculture, there was a dearth of running streams and rivers. This created a profound appreciation for water. Rights of access to springs and wells caused arguments that were settled for a price. The offer of water was considered an act of hospitality to travelers, another remembrance of the slavery in Egypt and years of wandering in the desert. A lack of water was one of the first issues faced after the exodus. Water flowing from a rock split open by Moses saved the people in their first moments of wandering. The stones that wept redeemed the journey.

Teresa of Avila wrote that there is no better representation of the spiritual life than water. Living in a city with significant water problems, she wrote of building aquifers, digging wells, and bringing water from one place to another as metaphors for the deepening process of prayer. Water that rises spontaneously from a spring is a gift from God. This is the water of life and of blessing. The element over which wars are fought is also the raw material of baptism. It cannot be privatized, owned, or withheld from others. Teresa also wrote of the drought, when God's presence seems far away and all efforts to access living water end in exhaustion. At such times the memory of water must suffice for the soul; a belief that the water will return and flow again is sufficient to carry us across a desert.

It is relatively easy to see the meaning of the clean waters of life that flow over the head of an infant presented for baptism. All of life is new. Creation is so fresh in the body of the baby that the ritual brings with it a surge of hope. Innocence is present, even after the bloody passage of birth. We are christening a child of God in the presence of the human community. Churches that practice infant baptism include in the sacramental ritual promises that the child will be accompanied on his or her faith journey, never alone.

The woundedness acknowledged in clean, white rituals is different from the concrete experience of the trauma survivor. Grief is both the baptismal water of trauma and the place of drought, the saline tears of knowing that life is irreversibly changed and the longing for sustenance in the soul's dryness. Trauma causes a loss of innocence that results in a profound experience of pain. Connections with others have been severed and trust is a challenge. Hesitation and caution have replaced the hope and celebration of new beginnings. The grief that pours out from the heart and soul in the tears of trauma creates a tricky passage that must be navigated with patience, care, and commitment.

Grief is a normal response to loss. There are many sources of loss in life, and some are more difficult than others. Loss is part of any process of change or growth; something familiar has to be left behind in the service of new life. There is at birth a loss of connection between mother and child that affects both of them; the child begins its own independent life without the protection of the womb, and the mother loses control as she surrenders the physiological oneness with her unborn child.

The gap between the world as one would expect it to be, and hope it to be, and reality is a continual loss that reverberates in some way through all creation myths. There is always a loss of innocence woven into those myths, a yearning for deeper knowledge that leads to some type of rupture with paradise. What is falls short of what was hoped for as truth. Dreams are broken, or must be abandoned, in light of reality. There is grief in those transitional spaces, a sense of bereavement in the knowledge that life can deal cruel blows and what is most precious to a person can be lost. That loss includes other people, health, time, hope, comfortable perceptions and understandings, and recognition of the fragility of life itself.

Parallel words for grief include hurt, harm, injury done by others, and, perhaps not surprisingly, wound. Grief can refer both to the damage or injury inflicted and the process of recovery from that injury. Grief is both a condition and a process; to carry grief is be the guardian of a deep wound. Grief lives in the body. It strikes at the bowels of human experience and works its way through each muscle and nerve. Tingling sensations and numbness are the nervous system's response to an overwhelming loss. The heart races and breath is constricted. Grief shuts down the body's normal appetites and desires; food has no appeal, rest is impossible, the sex drive is diminished. It is difficult to sleep. Concentration and focus are numbed; the mind seems to shut down in the face of great pain.

Grief can be elicited by both physical and spiritual losses, such as the loss of physical health or the experience of abandonment. The signs of grief are similar to the signs of stress, and indeed, bereavement is a major life stressor. The stress of grief braids together the pain of loss with the physiological response to strong emotion. The pain of grief is always embodied.

Grief deepens the knowledge that there are no guarantees in life, and that what we expect in the future may not come to pass. A woman who unexpectedly buried both of her parents in a short time found sleep very difficult. Sleeping pills proved ineffective for her. She decided to honor the rhythm of her grief by using the quiet of the night to be attentive to her grief. She spent the sleepless time journaling about her parents, the meaning of their lives, and her feelings about their deaths. She wrote and cried and prayed her way to the sunrises of an entire summer. She observed her grief until she felt ready to surrender to sleep. And then she welcomed the dreams and the memories they captured. There was a great deal of social support for her process. Her husband and family gave her the opportunity to work through her grief in a way that was healthy for her.

Not everyone has the wherewithal or support to work with their grief in that way. Grief has its own rhythms and purposes, which seldom follow the timeline or lead to the meaning the bereaved might choose. Like the trauma response, if the grieving process is perceived to be abnormal or a sign of intolerable disturbance, it becomes more difficult to respect its importance.

The psychologist William James wrote that "conversion is ego collapse at depth." The breakdown of the ego's power to organize, arrange, or understand is one of the most disconcerting elements of trauma and grief. As such, it can be a gateway to tremendous spiritual and emotional growth and conversion, or it can be only collapse without renewal.

There are many theories and articulations of the stages of grief that are applied to the grief that accompanies trauma. The most familiar is a model of five stages of grief: denial, anger, bargaining, depression, and acceptance. These stages are usually presented sequentially, but grief is not a linear or predictable experience. It is more accurately thought of as a cycle continually experienced and always in motion.

Grief, like spirituality, is fluid. The cycle of grief is affected by many influences and does not progress neatly. Grief is a process that involves the simultaneous presence of many different expressions. Grief passes through many living forms, sometimes in the same moment. There is an overlap in the stages, and they are visited more than once. Going through the cycle of grief deepens understanding and healing. Stages of grief, then, need to be understood as illustrative and interconnected, but not a guarantee of how the process unfolds for an individual or for a society.

The world has a maddening way of going on despite the profound grief experienced by an individual. The morning my father died, I stopped at a gas station to buy a cup of coffee. The young man at the counter was pleasant and energetic. As I was leaving he said, "Have a nice day." And I thought to myself "I am not only not going to have a nice day today, but I'm not sure that I will ever have a nice day again." I had entered the world of the bereaved whose suffering may not be immediately apparent to the world. I was actually rather shocked that the sun had come up that morning, and that there was still joy in the world and, in fact, that the world was continuing in its usual rhythm, oblivious to the great sadness of the night.

Invisible grief is encouraged in direct ways in North American culture. We cannot publicly give the splitting innards their voice to scream or to cry, to thrash and to demand mercy, without causing embarrassment to ourselves and others. External expression of the depth of grief, the keening, the screaming, and the physical collapse, are instead confused with an emotional breakdown. That, in fact, is exactly the role and meaning of grief; one is torn apart by the loss. The collapse of grief is not pathological; it is a conversion to a deeper reality.

Societies that have no rituals to announce mourning, that have no formal customs for dealing with bereavement and few community responses beyond the first few days after the loss (although, ironically, much more support will likely be needed later) demand a muted and quiet grief. The result is that a grieving person can wind up feeling very alone and isolated, which is a trauma in and of itself.

Isolated grief can easily become denial of the pain, on the part of both the person experiencing the loss and those around them. Denial is disbelief of the reality itself; it simply cannot—and will not—be true. Denial is common in life, and sometimes it serves as a temporary form of mercy. The first days of serious illness, overwhelming moments of trauma, or other circumstances where the situation is too powerful to be dealt with all at once are prime moments for denial. Its purpose is to carry a person to safety. Denial cannot continue, however, and becomes pathological when it stands in contrast to reality for too long a period of time.

Denial can be blinding in that it prevents the development of alternatives in the face of loss and requires enormous psychic energy. My neighbor who was dying of pancreatic cancer refused to believe that his illness was fatal. No amount of information from the doctors or from his family could convince him that a cure was impossible. He maintained to his last breath that he was going to beat the cancer. His denial of the reality of his condition made it impossible for the family to talk with him about his death or to say goodbye. The denial deepened the family's grief because so much was left unsaid.

Denial also keeps private trauma that should be exposed; the severity of an abuse situation, for example, is denied or explained away, thus truncating the hope of healing. Admitting the reality of the injury would possibly prevent future abuse, even as it would give voice to the grief of the victim. Denial only deepens the tragedy.

Anger at loss is a necessary part of the grief experience. Rage against circumstances leads to a desire for revenge. Anger at a person for dying is a paradoxical emotion summed up well by a young widow who said to me about her husband, "If he weren't already dead, I would kill him for causing me this much pain." There is a need to blame, to find someone who can be held responsible for the loss. Blaming the victim or someone who should have helped the victim comes into being through anger at the circumstances of the loss.

It is in this part of the process that careful analysis of what could have been done differently is carried out, sometimes to torturous degrees. This is the "what if" or "if only" stage of grief, when victims and the people around them second guess on the premise that they will feel more protected if some error by the victim is uncovered. If only she hadn't gone for a walk so early in the morning, or exercised during pregnancy, or married that man, she would have been fine. If only she had had more faith. If only I had not gone to work that day, or listened to him more carefully, or paid more attention to the pain. Things would be different, if only I had tried harder. No matter how much analysis is done of circumstances, mistakes made, or opportunities lost in the trauma, the events themselves are not reversed. What could be part of memorial meaning-making becomes instead an exercise of denial and rage.

For survivors of trauma, the question of why something happened provokes anger, if only at the seeming meaninglessness of the circumstances. The search for a sense of reason or explanation often either comes up empty or leads to more questions about the nature of life. I have known at least four different families whose ancestors missed the Titanic. The dates and the details of the stories do not necessarily square with historic facts, including the grandmother who was immigrating to America on the Carpathia, which picked up the survivors on its way to Europe from New York harbor. The power of the story is the meaning it gives to other difficult life events. Generally the conclusion is that the ancestor was "spared for a purpose." The rest of the person's life and difficulties are then understood within the context of that purpose or special mission from God.

Ideas like this surface in public often. When there is an accident or a disaster, there are always eerie coincidences of people who would have been there if they hadn't missed the boat, stayed home sick, or been stuck in traffic. God's hand reached down and saved them. I do not doubt that if I were in the position of the survivor, I would be thanking God for mercy. But there is always a question that haunts the storytelling—what of those who were not saved, who made the launch of the ship, who were at the point of impact? Did God choose for them to die for a purpose?

The more haunting, perplexing question is the "why not" of one's own survival, most especially, why did I not die when others did? Why did I survive, why didn't I save more people, how can I live with myself knowing what others have gone through? The questions that arise from this sense of guilt on the part of survivors cannot be resolved in a rational way because they are not questions based on logic. They are questions that cry out from the depth of loss and cover its meaning. The grief at the loss of others and the unforgettable knowledge of what happened to them causes immense pain.

This is an occupational hazard for people whose work brings them into dangerous circumstances or causes them to see more than their share of human suffering. The question comes up in times of war, or along the highway when someone has died in an accident and someone else has lived. It is linked to a perceived failure to affect the outcome of events, the powerlessness of the doctor, or the minister, or the human rights worker.

The need to find a reason for injury or survival is a defensive strategy. If only there is a reason, or a mistake can be identified and judgment made, the reality of lost control and powerlessness can be avoided. The reality that this can and does happen to anyone sinks in when the unspeakable is witnessed or directly experienced. The vulnerability to which that reality leads calls for reestablishing a connection that is redemptive, even if that connection is still in the hope of changing reality.

And so, we bargain with God, with ourselves, with each other. I will do anything, change anything, if there can be a different outcome. Our attempts to bargain in life are also ways of trying to regain power in the hope that loss can be avoided. These deals are usually struck in silence, a promise to give anything if the pain of the loss can be avoided. I will promise God that I will give money to the poor if a favor is performed. The favor can be anything from restoring a relationship to resurrection of the dead.

Bargaining is way to manage the grief of the uncertainty provoked by loss; if I do not yet know how things are going to work out, I will attempt to influence the outcome in some way. If there is a truth that I am denying, then bargaining is a means of working through the layers of self-deception to embrace reality.

Ultimately, the bargaining will fail because there is no way to reverse the loss. Nothing can change reality and so a way to live with it must be found. Initially, the way of coping may seem to be more suffering. No amount of pleading or wishing for something to change will work. There are many circumstances, including victimization or death, when there is a compelling ache to offer our own lives if reality can somehow be changed. Yet none of us can reverse the reality of trauma and its losses by trying to change events that have already occurred. I cannot offer my life in place of another, nor can I take away the other's pain.

With the loss of bargaining power comes total vulnerability. And with the vulnerability comes another choice in the grieving process—how to live in the presence and reality of the loss.

Depression is often listed as a stage of grief, but it is not a universal experience. While grief and depression share common physiological and emotional symptoms such as feelings of sadness, frustration, and hopelessness, they are not the same. Feelings of grief are episodic, not continual. The sadness may come over a person like a wave that then retreats for a period of time. Unlike depression, grief does not cause damage to self-esteem or lead to pervasive feelings of worthlessness and guilt. Those feelings are at the core of depression and they are continuous.

When the husband and father in a family of four died in a car accident, the youngest child was six months old. At the funeral, people commented that the baby was probably the luckiest of the children, because she would not remember her father, and certainly would not experience the same grief as the older children.

Within a year, however, the healthy, robust baby was growing very slowly and had fallen behind in her psychosocial development. Terrified, the mother took the child to doctors who ruled out many possibilities. The final diagnosis was failure to thrive. The mother loved and cared for her child, yet the baby who was thought to be blessed with the power to forget absorbed the loss and stress in the family. Her growth was slowed by the family's grief. Her listlessness and lack of curiosity were non-verbal cries for help. Work with the child and the family reversed the symptoms and the little girl recovered.

The equivalent of failure to thrive in adults can be the depression that sets in as a response to grief. Depression is more than feeling sad or down; it is a loss of vitality and a lack of growth. The feelings of hopelessness, frustration, self-pity, powerlessness, being out of control, and perhaps wanting to die are all manifested in the body and experienced as the draining away of life force. Depression as an element of grief is hard to endure because of its impact on energy. In depression, even the simplest actions become overwhelming. The details that must be tended in life (and situations leading to grief bring details in their wake) feel impossibly complicated.

The root word for mourning is believed by some scholars to be *meur*, to die or wither away Depression is that process of withering, the loss of energy for day-to-day activities. It is mourning at its most grave. Suicidal or other self-destructive thoughts and behavior are not uncommon among grieving people who become depressed. The perception that it is better to be dead than to face the pain of a loss, or the reality of a world in which such horrible events happen, should be listened to carefully and taken seriously by those around a depressed person.

It is always wise to enlist professional help in situations of depression because it is a medical condition that can be effectively treated. When the depression lifts, there may still be profound feelings of grief. There will, however, be increased energy to integrate those feelings.

The stage of grief referred to as acceptance brings with it the realization that the reality cannot be denied or changed. Since trauma can be the result of events that are unacceptable by anyone's standards, coming to some resolution of the grief does not mean that the causes of it are any less painful. Rape, domestic violence, and other causes of trauma are unacceptable forms of human behavior. Nonetheless, for the person who has suffered immense loss as the result of that behavior, naming the reality is important. Acceptance is not something that can be rushed or ever considered to be the final goal. It is the beginning of a different way of living with reality. It is a part of the cycle of grief and of life, a reaching for the presence of love in others that nurtures new meanings.

ONE OF THE MORE CONTROVERSIAL historic social service movements in the United States was that of the orphan trains. From 1850 until 1929, children living in poverty, hunger, violence, and otherwise without adult care were sent west on trains to be adopted by families. Some of the youngsters knew the parents they were leaving behind, some were taken as very small children. The intent was to remove them from urban squalor and give them care not possible in the cities of the east.

Announcements were made at the primarily Midwestern towns along the train line that the children would be arriving and could be chosen for adoption. Minimal investigation was done of the homes where the children would be placed. At each stop, the children were displayed. It was not unusual for potential adoptive parents to feel the child's muscles and assess what type of work he or she would be able to perform. If children were not chosen, they were taken to the next town. Siblings were separated, and some weak or sickly children traveled the length of the train lines, were examined, and were consistently rejected for adoption.

Many of the children found good homes. But many others were adopted only for the labor they could provide. They were treated harshly and never given an opportunity to claim the pain of the orphan train experience. Children who had been taken away from their parents were encouraged to "forget" their parents, and not allowed to speak of their loss.

Having been part of the orphan train program was a cause for shame and the children grew up with such a profound fear of abandonment (and many of them were, in fact, abandoned a second or third time) that the grief of the separations from parents and siblings had no outlet. Oral histories taken fifty years after the last orphan train revealed that the grief of the orphan train children was closely held inside or consciously ignored. Many of those children discovered the intensity of their grief only later in life when threatened again with separation. The fear of abandonment that had ruled their lives made any goodbye enough to rip apart their souls.

The adults did not necessarily make the connection to the grief of their childhood because those ancient losses were sequestered, impacted, and unnamed. To speak of the grief seemed disloyal to the people who had tried to help them. To not speak of the grief was to be ruled by its power, either by trying to throw the switch on all emotion, or through substance abuse and other forms of denial.

The complex history of the orphan trains is arousing new interest in scholars and social service agencies struggling with the desire to avoid tragic mistakes that happen with the best intentions. That so much pain came out of something intended to alleviate suffering is a grief of its own.

Families and entire cultures can attempt to keep their grief impacted, particularly if the loss seems to involve any kind of shame. Suicides that are recorded as accidental deaths bury the possibility of appropriate grief and anger under the guise of kindness, of trying to spare people the pain of the truth. Tucked away in family secrets and social denial, the sequestered grief does not cease to exist; it simply goes underground.

It is a common misperception that children do not grieve for things that happened before they were born. Yet grief has a way of flowing from one generation to the next like mother's milk; it is absorbed and made part of oneself without knowledge of what it contains. Within families, the hidden traumas sow inexplicable grief as an inheritance. The grief engendered by early loss of a parent or sibling has been shown to be carried into the second generation, even if there was no direct experience of loss by those children. The patterns of life and the sorrows inflicted by the loss are hard to erase, and they find their way into an expectation of life that is consistent with hidden grief. The children of the children learn that grief is a template for living. This is a lesson wordlessly transferred yet completely understood: be careful in the world, because loss is everywhere. The transferred message of care from other trauma survivors is slightly different: the world cannot be trusted, because danger is everywhere.

THERE IS A HIERARCHY in the expectations of what constitutes acceptable grief, a hierarchy that parallels judgments about how traumatic events should affect people. The judgment is strengthened by largely individualized assumptions that people should grieve in particular ways for particular events; the widow should grieve more than the mother-in-law, the children more than the grandchildren, those present at the event more than those who are watching it on television.

Yet those pyramids and expectations provide little opportunity for an appropriate experience of grief and can add layers to the suffering of the bereaved. Why should I be so upset by this death? Why is she so undone at the funeral of someone she hardly knows? Why does this small loss feel so catastrophic? Why can't I get over it? Why does this trauma that happened to someone else cause such pain to me?

It is so easy to judge those not seen as being directly connected to the events, or experiencing a depth of feeling out of proportion with the relationship that was known by others. Yet, as with prior trauma, we have no way of knowing what grief is waiting to be claimed in the life of another person. A small rain can flood saturated ground. There is a need to trust the message of the grief, to receive it and to recognize the right of all people to grieve in their own way and time. The current loss is rarely all that is involved in the heart's response.

It is important to remember that we grieve not just the past, but the future as well. The woman who miscarries does not lose a clump of cells gestated to a certain point. She loses the baby, the child, the graduating senior. The people whose names are listed on the Vietnam Memorial would be grandparents by now. Future generations are lost in every war.

Victor Frankl's life work as a psychiatrist was deeply influenced by his experience in a concentration camp. He pointed out that human beings have a fundamental need to believe in the future, not just a hope for one's individual future but an embrace of future possibilities for humanity. If that belief is lost, it is impossible to live well in the present, and perhaps impossible to live at all.

Frankl observed that some people survived the concentration camps by thinking about how they were going to tell the story once they were released. That preparation for storytelling kept alive the belief not only that the person rehearsing the story would survive but also that there would be subsequent generations to hear the story. Given the murderous intentions of the Nazis, this was no small leap of faith. That belief provided the distance and sense of empowerment that made it possible to survive the horrible indignities of the camp—and to survive knowing exactly what had happened.

When trauma destroys belief in the future, there is no container for grief and so it remains unprocessed and grows in power. The fear of grief caused by events can foreclose the future as rapidly as the events themselves. As in other traumatic circumstances, any reminder of the loss and anything that awakens the grief is to be avoided. It requires courage to live in the presence of grief, particularly if there is a lack of supportive relationships. One of the goals of the grieving process is to internalize relationships and people with whom there was an external relationship. The embodiment of that shift is in the embrace of new possibilities that carry the best of what was lost into the future. This creates the option to feel whole again without feeling guilty.

There is a line from the play *I Never Sang for My Father* that expresses a basic truth: "Death ends a life, but not a relationship." The relationship with what was lost continues internally, with emotions parallel to what existed in the external relationship. This was illustrated for me by a widow whose husband sometimes appeared in her dreams with a critique of her investment decisions. Her standard dream response to him was that she wasn't going to take advice from someone who had been dead as long as he had. She would take her stock tips from people who were capable of reading the *Wall Street Journal* because they are still alive, thank you very much. The relationship continued at a level of dialogue and discord within her dreams that was consistent with her prior relationship with her husband.

Relationships continue beyond the grave. If a relationship was one of great pain, grieving for that relationship is a complex process, because hope of the situation ever improving has been extinguished by the death. Hence, grief brings to the surface unresolved pain that can be so powerful that it is avoided all together. With that avoidance comes a lack of hope for the future.

Without the experience of grief there can be no letting into consciousness the reality of relationships, events, and their losses, and so no surrender to the new reality. Without the surrender, there can be no imagination. Grief and imagination are wedded to each other. It is impossible to envision a future life without working through the truth that another reality is constantly being left behind.

Walter Bruggeman has articulated this link in his book *Prophetic Imagination.* He points out that the prophets of the Hebrew Scriptures expressed profound grief for the losses of their people. The texts contain long lamentations about what has been wrought by lack of fidelity and alienation not only from God, but from a basic sense of identity. Jeremiah says, "My heart breaks within me, my grief is ever present." He is naming a situation that he believes did not have to have come about, preventable disaster that has now devastated the people.

The pattern of the prophets is to invoke the memory of God's fidelity as a response to their grief. Remembering the history of a people creates the possibility for a new way of understanding and living—a way of imagining a new heaven and a new earth. Imagination can only be born out of grief for what is and has been. As painful as grief can be, if respected and experienced in a supportive context, it renews the possibility of a future.

Grief acknowledges that a link has been severed. Living into that truth frees the soul to believe again in the future and to imagine a new possibility. It is familiar to speak of grief as letting go when it fact the process is one of letting in to consciousness the importance of what has been lost and to weep it into a new form, like water that shifts the shape of the land.

It is the process of grief giving way to imagination that is at the heart of transforming the traumatic experience. Those who have experienced trauma of any kind cannot move into the future without the acknowledgment of the memory, and genuine mourning that such pain exists in the world. There is deep grief in looking at the suffering of the people of God and recognizing how little can be controlled or alleviated in a single lifetime. The grief at knowing the depth of the wound is threatening in that safe understandings and meanings fall away. Grief is a liminal process filled with the unknown and experienced as being completely without structure. There is seldom much concrete, external evidence that what feels like inner bedlam will blossom into imagination or creativity.

The prophetic role is to hold close to the memory of the fidelity of God when all else is lost. Access to that memory is intrinsically connected to the deepest lament; to fall into the pain is to know that God's concrete presence is not a reversal of events, but a claiming of the life that remains. That life is coaxed into being through the compassionate understanding and care of others who are not afraid to look at the mystery of loss and simply let it be without explanation.

The greatest act of faith for those encountering grief is to stand in its presence and make no attempts to explain it away. Only then is grief freed to reveal its imaginative possibilities, the most vital of which is the desire to love again.

A Grief beyond Telling

I WENT BACK TO SCHOOL WHEN MY CHILDREN WERE THREE and five, ages when nurturance is immediate and intense. My life revolved around the needs of the children. They were always present in my mind.

The first night of class, the professor asked each of us to introduce ourselves and describe why we were taking a counseling course. One of the women introduced herself as Charlotte and added, "I am a bereaved parent." She had lost her only child when he was in his early twenties. He was killed by a drunk driver. She was taking the class as part of a graduate program to prepare her to counsel other bereaved parents.

Her words took my breath away, first, because she had testified to the possibility that parents do lose their children, and second because I wondered why the loss still seemed so fresh to her. Since I could not bear to even think about the possibility that something could happen to my own children and I felt I could not deal with the intensity of the woman's pain, I avoided her for a long time.

We were in several classes together and I gradually came to know her as a woman of great courage. I learned that my instinct to stay away from her was typical. I had temporarily joined the ranks of those who approached her cautiously. Her very presence embodied fears of the worst kinds of suffering and unspeakable loss. There is a taboo against bringing the word or experience into the light. If she would only be silent, the rest of us could feel safe and protected from the unpredictability of life.

Her grief was a threat that evoked in others a complex fear and heartbreak that made it seem best to avoid her altogether. One of her greatest pains was that people she had known for years were afraid to mention the name of her child for fear of "upsetting" her. She was the person who first alerted me to the perils of predictable stages and time-lines for grief. The expectations embedded in some of the literature can be devastating if one's experience is different. The process called "normal" or uncomplicated grief—and I have yet to see grief that didn't exist in a complicated way—is presented as the standard. Any deviation from that process leads to external and internal judgment. What is wrong with her? What is wrong with me?

There are experiences of grief that are not pathological— they are simply different. Charlotte found that most material about grief assumed the loss of a parent, spouse, or relative of one's own generation or older. That her own grief felt so qualitatively different confused her and frightened others. Her quest for understanding and validation took her to three different therapists. Each one labeled her grief as inappropriate and urged her to get on with her life. The fourth therapist admitted that she didn't fully understand the process of grief under the particular circumstances, but that, according to Charlotte, "she was willing to listen and she was not afraid of me." Together they found a way to bring her some relief. An essential part of that relief was hearing that she was not deficient because her grief flowed in a different channel than that described in the standard literature.

Charlotte was experiencing traumatic grief, a grief that follows a loss so devastating that it evokes the trauma response. The intrusive, avoidance, and arousal symptoms that are part of grief are especially powerful if the grief results from an experience of sudden or unexpected events. The faces of people standing at the edge of the Indian Ocean and staring at the water whose tsunami had taken their loved ones was a powerful representation of traumatic grief. In the space of a few minutes, their worlds had been smashed and swept away. Their disbelieving hearts could not immediately comprehend such devastating loss. The people were stunned, they were numb, they had profound grief and immediate physical needs. Their unfocused eyes looking at the sea reflected a grief that would have no words for a long, long time.

TRAUMATIC GRIEF IS COMMON when the death or other loss comes with shocking suddenness, or as a result of events that are so painful that the events themselves may be denied. A suicide becomes an accidental drowning, a violent death a terrible accident. Denial of the circumstances of the death precludes the possibility of transforming the relationship and so impact the grief. The death of a loved one who has been a perpetrator of abuse can cause traumatic grief because the troubled history may still be held in silence, and the survivor must deal with recurrent trauma symptoms as well as feelings of grief at the loss. Traumatic grief can also follow a long, difficult death. For the caregiver, it may have been necessary to keep his or her own feelings hidden in order to be of service to the dying person. When the death occurs, those feelings rise to the surface along with a potential loss of identity and purpose.

Denial of traumatic events themselves forecloses the grief process and leads to impacted grief. This kind of grief, like material dissociated from memory, lives in its own protected space within the body and mind. It cannot come to the surface, but its presence presses against consciousness and sometimes causes damage to the surrounding tissues of relationships. Grief that is impacted between skin and bone without expression or legitimacy pushes toward the surface, but there is a strong message that the grief must be kept out of sight for emotional survival. If there is no opportunity for expression at the time of the loss, impacted grief can become disconnected from its source. The awakening of grief is then confusing and traumatic in its own right.

Pockets of impacted grief contribute to depression and a loss of energy. Those pockets sometimes spill their contents only when another loss is experienced. Impacted grief is a receptor for other losses. Grief finds its like within the soul. Grief over early losses in life can present itself in a powerful way when later grief is experienced. Impacted grief is the parallel to what Pierre Janet called "frozen memory." It lives in the body rigidly, and it reveals itself in ways that are current, not past. This is the grief of the hidden lover, the soldier who acted against his conscience, the mother of the murder victim or of the criminal killed by lethal injection, the survivor of long-term abuse. Its presence and power are given no legitimacy.

The primary difference between traumatic grief and more typical grief is that in the latter the symptoms are related to separation and the desire to be reunited with what has been lost. The emotional process of grief allows for a reconnection with the person who has been lost through recognition of memory, transformation of the relationship, and the freedom to find pleasure in other meaningful relationships. The symptoms of traumatic grief are fueled by a separation that in and of itself is so traumatic that it is difficult to even admit to the death itself. Signs of traumatic grief include recurrent intrusive thoughts about the person who has died, and particularly, the circumstances of the death.

At the same time, there can be denial of the circumstances or reality of the death. Society often supports keeping silent about traumatic death because of the mistaken assumption that to mention the death to survivors will bring the loss to consciousness. Since the survivor is extremely aware of the loss, failure to mention it actually increases the stigma and isolation, and therefore the pain of the trauma. There may be a need to avoid all reminders of what was lost. The traumatic separation evokes rage, guilt, and a desire for revenge. There may be intense rage, as well as jealousy of others who have not been subjected to the same experience.

Social withdrawal is common in all forms of grief, but in traumatic grief it is a greater impairment. Feelings of futility about the future, avoidance of any activities, places, or people that are reminders of the loss, and despair about ever feeling normal again are stronger in those experiencing traumatic grief. The resulting trauma symptoms cause significant life impairment.

The healing of traumatic grief requires that the symptoms of intrusion, avoidance, and arousal be acknowledged and stabilized. The trauma symptoms need to be addressed before engaging in the process of working with the grief itself. In a significant way, the trauma symptoms keep the grief at bay; to stabilize the symptoms is to open the possibility for healing of the grief. Then the transformation of grief into a process of living again begins to occur.

Traumatic grief is not transitional, in that clinging to the grief may be a way of retaining a connection with what has been lost. As with all trauma, the existence of the wound speaks to a survival instinct. Mobilizing those desires toward healing is a sensitive and lengthy process. To give up the symptoms of traumatic grief is to make an adaptation to an unacceptable reality. It recognizes that there are irreconcilable, unresolvable losses in life. What caused the losses and the trauma created by them cannot be undone, no matter how much energy is devoted to examining the whys and hows of the experience.

Traumatic grief has a particularly strong component of guilt that makes it seem disloyal to feel better and go on with life. The pain itself can be understood as a way of keeping the lost person alive; to let go of the suffering is to erase the existence of what was lost. Like water, the grief sustains life even as it carries the potential of death. Proper containment and management of symptoms creates a sense of safety.

Charlotte found balance through a therapeutic process that was expansive enough to allow her not only to hold her trauma and grief but also to help her envision a future. That type of accompaniment relies on a basic willingness to meet a grieving person on his or her own terms. All forms of trauma and grief are soothed and potentially transformed by the presence of a compassionate witness.

Witnesses have to be willing to endure the pain of another person without comforting themselves by trying to explain the pain away. It is pointless and potentially damaging to provide spiritual explorations of why something happened or offer words intended to comfort that instead deepen the pain. Another woman who lost her child was told at the wake "God loves you very much to give you this kind of suffering," to which she replied, "How about if

God loves me a bit less and I get my son back?" The person who offered those words of comfort never made that mistake again.

Witnesses to trauma must be willing to step into the void of having no answers, solutions, or understanding of something that cannot and will not be explained away. What is of importance and comfort is to honor the beliefs of the bereaved person, which at the time of trauma may be elusive. With the permission of the other person, all of the rituals and sacred healing processes can be brought to the traumatic grief as a resource. But they cannot be imposed. What is needed is support in the process of surrendering life for life, a holding and honoring of the unspeakable.

Charlotte used her experience to develop a support group of people trained to come to the local hospital emergency room and assist others who had lost a loved one under sudden and tragic circumstances. As one who had experienced the loss of her son in a car accident, she understood the needs of survivors to see the body, to know the full story of the injuries, and to be empowered to make decisions about the rituals of burial. Charlotte's work sprang from her experience of isolation; she did not want anyone else to suffer that experience. The most compassionate witnesses of all are the ones who have shared similar experiences and are living testimony to the possibility, indeed the reality, of survival.

Fire

Mary Harris Jones was born in Cork, Ireland, on May 1, 1830. Ireland at that time was a country under violent repression. As an adult Mary would describe having seen British soldiers march through town carrying the heads of Irish freedom fighters. The great hunger was soon to follow. Mary's family left Ireland on what came to be known as a "coffin ship" because so many passengers died on the vessels that were their only hope of escaping the famine.

Because passage to Canada was cheaper than passage to the United States, Mary's family was among the many Irish who disembarked in Canada. Mary went to school in Toronto and then moved to Michigan where she became a school teacher for a few years. After that she worked as a seamstress in Chicago, where she observed the stark difference between the life of her employers and that of the workers she saw on the streets.

Mary Harris married and moved to Tennessee where, in one harrowing week in 1867, she lost her husband and their four small children to a Yellow Fever epidemic. She moved back to Chicago, and a few months after her arrival, she stood in Lake Michigan to escape the flying embers from the Great Chicago Fire. It was after the fire that Mary became involved in the labor movement.

With all of her personal experience of repression, tragedy, death, and loss, this displaced woman from Ireland became known as "Mother Jones—the Miners' Angel." As Mother Jones, she became a powerful force in the struggle for just wages and safe working conditions. She was so effective as a labor organizer that a district attorney in Virginia referred to this tiny, elderly lady as "the most dangerous woman in America." She led miners' wives and children in marches to protest the conditions in the mines. When asked where she lived, Mother Jones replied, "Wherever there is a fight."

Mother Jones traveled around the country telling the stories of the miners, including those machine-gunned to death in a 1914 strike in Colorado. She took offense at being called a humanitarian, much preferring the title of "hell raiser." Mother Mary Harris Jones was a woman whose anger flared in the face of injustices. She spoke with passion on behalf of people who had no voice, especially children laboring in unsafe conditions. Her personal experience fueled an activism that alleviated the suffering of others.

Having lost everything more than once, Mother Jones contributed to the improvement of conditions for all workers in America. She knew the meaning of holy wrath. Her personal experience and its resulting anger were transformed into a fight for the rights of others. Mary Jones, a woman whose personal suffering could easily have led her to withdrawal and depression, instead chose to side with the living. The bereaved woman became Mother to those most in need of a passionate companion. Mother Jones had a favorite saying that summarizes the way she lived after the

Chicago Fire: "Pray for the dead, fight like hell for the living." Her mantra offers a way to envision transformation of personal anger into meaningful work on behalf of others: recognize what cannot be changed, fight to bring about a different reality. Anger is excellent fuel for that type of conversion.

IT IS IMPOSSIBLE TO WRITE ABOUT THE ROLE OF ANGER in recovery from trauma without acknowledging that anger is a greatly misunderstood and feared energy. There is enough interest in defining and managing anger to create between six million and eleven million Internet sites, depending on the search engine used.

Anger is an emotion that is as natural to humanity as fear, joy, or sadness. It is a natural response to threat. Anger and injury are essentially connected. When wounded, animals become angry and frightened in order to protect themselves and survive. Human anger serves a similar purpose; it is meant to mobilize us for definition and survival, not to cripple us with demands for revenge or shame at its existence. Anger can be the protective crust of a tender wound.

For some trauma survivors, anger is the most available emotion. Feeling and expressing anger, whether appropriately or not, protects the heart from feeling its pain and grief. Recognizing the source of anger requires admission of the pain or threat that provokes it. Anger can feel destabilizing when connected with grievous pain. Though anger is not categorically violent, to other trauma survivors it feels that way because it is perceived as being untamed and undigested. Anger is perceived to have the power to blow apart any adjustment that has been made to the trauma.

Anger can be linked with fears of abandonment; if I show my anger, I will be left alone. Anger is feared because of a perception that it destroys relationships or leads to some type of violence. The traumatized have often been on the receiving end of blind rage, out-of-control anger that is violent and harmful to others. To feel one's own anger is to potentially identify with the rage of the oppressor. Anger needs to be differentiated from the rage, aggression, and violence that may have been part of trauma. Ironically, these potentially dangerous expressions can be born of anger that is unrecognized and untended at its source and so becomes a habitual means of defense. Yet it can become quite difficult to differentiate the energy; at the first signs of anger, traumatized persons may fear becoming as violent or out of control as those who victimized them. Great energy is expended to keep the anger hidden because of the fear it invokes.

Like impacted grief, anger needs to be respected and used as energy for change. No one needs to die or be diminished in the face of anger. Anger is an appropriate response to dehumanization, betrayal, or abuse. It is both protective and expressive. Yet to people who have experienced trauma, anger is more often seen as threat rather than as potentially healing energy.

It is interesting to note that in a society filled with road rage, violent imagery, and more deaths from handguns than any other country on earth, it is considered bad form to express anger directly and appropriately. Displaced anger is common in daily life and is often directed toward others with unreasonable intensity. This is the anger that takes people by surprise and provokes a like response.

For all the free-floating rage in the culture, calling someone with legitimate complaints an "angry person" is dismissive, as if the content of the anger is not worthy of being heard and the person herself is to be avoided. This charge of "being angry" is frequently leveled against people who are coming into an awareness of their own suffering and pain. An acquaintance of mine is fond of saying that "there is nothing worse than an angry feminist." And he means it. Unfortunately, the sentence also works when other people or groups are substituted for "feminist."

One of the most explosive people I have ever met admitted to me that he was afraid of being thought of as an angry person. So he swallowed indignity after indignity until he reached a point where his anger burst forth with the velocity of a typhoon. His own worst fears were realized; he was not just considered an angry person, he scared people half to death. It was a tremendous step in his growth and relationships with others when he learned that appropriate expression of anger is possible to integrate into daily life.

THE POSSIBILITY OF LISTENING to the pain beneath the anger or perhaps changing attitudes in the presence of its truth is eclipsed by the judgment that anger is a sign of irrationality. Like those who suffer deep grief, the person with obvious anger is something of a threat. The danger exists on several levels: fear of being hurt by the angry person, the awakening of one's own anger, and the possibility of needing to change in the face of the truth revealed by the anger of another person.

To find expression for the immense anger felt as part of trauma requires challenging some fundamental beliefs about anger. Admitting to the anger caused by trauma is part of the revision of one's sense of self that is required for healing. The experience of powerlessness and threat changes one's understanding of living in the world. The accompanying vulnerability means that it is no longer possible to regard oneself as immortal or protected from the dangers of life.

The depth of anger connected with trauma causes a shifting of perception of how one interacts with the world. For someone who has struggled to work for peace or reconciliation, anger feels particularly disconcerting. Anger provoked by trauma can be especially threatening because it feels out of control, as if, once again, there is perceived helplessness over the situation and one's internal response.

Because trauma ruptures a basic understanding and expectation of the world, it is always a source of anger. Major expectations of life have been violated by events and their sequels. Trauma is a profound disappointment in the reality that, as the Buddha reportedly noted, suffering is the only promise that life keeps.

Since anger is one of the eight deadly sins, there is a certain inhibition about following the example of the psalmist and ranting at God for the sense of abandonment and betrayal brought on by trauma. The scriptural template of lament is one in which anger leads to conversion and an understanding of divine presence. Job's declaration that "I know my redeemer lives" is spoken from the top of a dung heap after torrents of anger at his suffering. The lesson he learns from his anger is that God, in fact, is not indifferent, though the expression of God's care may fall far below Job's expectations.

To rage at God requires a significant departure from the image of God as one who wounds as means of punishment. The underlying theme that there must be a grand plan or reason for who lives and who dies on the individual and family level strengthens the idea that trauma victims have contributed to or caused their own difficulties. St. Monica offered advice to the women of Hippo to avoid domestic violence by not inciting the men around them. If the women behaved well, they would not be beaten. Abused children and survivors of adult trauma sometimes make decisions to be really, really good in the hope that God will protect them as a reward for their good behavior. The hope of making things right through good behavior is hard to reconcile with the depth of an ongoing, traumatic injury. The trauma is then cast as proof of failure.

Organized religion has frequently contributed to the problems of domestic violence by emphasizing the need for obedience, a hierarchy of authority, and the sanctity of marriage regardless of how horrendous its circumstances might be. Encouraging victims to suffer quietly or offer up their pain for the sake of holiness not only belittles the anger of targets of abuse, it threatens their survival. It is for this reason that 12-step and other recovery groups emphasize spirituality over religion; spirituality and God are both freed from the harmful social code and doctrines of a religious tradition that encourages violence against the innocent. Spirituality calls anger and oppression by name as an act of faith; the anger itself is holy.

Anger is the energy of transformation. St. Thomas Aquinas said that anger is "the name of a passion." He went on to write that all human passions can become substitutes for God and so require moderation. The passion of anger is not an end in itself; it is part of the process of life that embraces and responds to reality. Like the alchemist's fire, anger changes the elements of life without destroying them. It is possible to create something of beauty with the fire of anger, but only if there is enough space created within to let the fire breathe.

The power of anger after trauma is such that it feels like something destructive that will blow apart the mechanisms of coping and relationship. When properly appropriated, however, anger, instead of demanding and fueling revenge, is productive energy that creates a new understanding of the world. Anger, like grief, must run its course along pathways and time periods that are not of our choosing. Anger, however, cannot become healing or transformative if left on its own. It has to be respected and invited into consciousness before it will share its power. The real danger of anger is not the feeling itself, but the ways in which the attempt to contain it hollow out one's humanity rather than enhance it. Anger becomes destructive when it is used to diminish instead of serving as passion for change.

Fear and anger together leave a residue that can draw very strict lines between symbol and person, feelings that are acceptable to admit and rage beyond telling, truth and blatant denial that crimes and survival are even part of human life. It is a rigid and not uncommon system of keeping the world manageable when there is so much complexity, nuance, and mystery in life. It is a system born of rage. This foundational violence exists on personal as well as on political levels.

I HAVE KNOWN ENOUGH VICTIMS OF SEXUAL VIOLENCE to have strong opinions about perpetrators of such violence. I am particularly harsh about the type of denial of reality that seeks to blame the victim, or dismiss the depth of the injury to the victims by pointing out that perpetrators have their own pain. While intellectually I know that to be true, on the level of emotion I have been inclined to find it less complicated to keep anger, and yes, a certain hatred alive toward the perpetrators.

I have declined opportunities to be involved in a prison ministry at Sing Sing because, though I pass by it often on the train to New York, it has felt too complicated to engage with prisoners who I know have committed crimes against women. It challenges my impossible desire to keep the world divided between victims and perpetrators, those worthy of mercy and those who inspire thoughts of revenge. I don't readily admit those divisions, even to myself, but there is no question that they are there, like the remnants of a child's view of the world that casts what is incomprehensible into the protective category of "not human and worthy of rage." What such a stance lacks in humanity is made up for by convenience and protection against the meaning of both anger and pain.

I was, then, a somewhat reluctant participant in a visit to a Latin American jail. A tall, soft-spoken lawyer invited me to go with him and observe as he talked to some of the prisoners about their cases. A former public defender in the United States, the lawyer had come to Latin America to help those who are powerless within an overwhelming system that breeds injustice. He uses his skills to help those most on the margins of society; he takes the cases of those who have no advocate.

The jails are filled both with innocent people and individuals for whom the violence of the society has included their own actions and breaking of boundaries. No matter what the reason for the incarceration, no one should live in such prison conditions. As in most prison systems around the world, there is no food provided to the prisoners by the government. The food, blankets, or anything else that is needed to stay alive must be provided by others or purchased with a meager allotment from the government, an allotment that is inadequate and often not available. When the government is broke, which it often is, there are no other provisions for purchasing food for oneself. The meeting of basic needs is dependent on the kindness of family members or other outsiders and the small amount of money that can be made working in small industries within the jail. The jail is a small village behind walls. Laundry hangs from a line stretched across the courtyard of the jail.

The prisoners make furniture to supplement their allotments and provide for themselves when there are no outside resources. It is possible to go to the prison or the nearby plaza and shop for furniture made by prisoners. A number on each piece identifies the person who made it. Potential buyers then go to the jail and bargain with the prisoner over the price of the furniture. It is clearly a buyer's market. The danger involved in furniture making is evident in the rough bandages wrapped around hands and arms that got too close to a saw or other tool and must heal without medical attention.

The guard takes our passports as we enter. He has a gentle face but carries a gun lest I forget that there is violence in every aspect of this place, including the poverty of the women trying to survive by cooking for the prisoners. They will be paid with the pittance of the inmates who build the chairs in the plaza. I wonder for a minute about my passport as I keep walking into the interior of the jail. I believe that I have entered a small corner of hell.

I follow the lawyer into a tiny room with a table and four chairs. The first prisoner to enter the room is a man in jail for rape. He impregnated his fifteen-year-old stepdaughter. As he walks into the room, I feel a flash of anger. I listen carefully to the conversation between him and the lawyer. The man will plead guilty, a new possibility under a revised criminal code. "The crime is very serious," the lawyer says, and the man shakes his head in agreement. "You will be in jail for twenty years." The man understands that. He is unconvinced that he does not need to pay off the judge in order to make his plea, for that is the way of the system.

There is a short discussion between the man and the lawyer, who explains again the change in the laws that facilitate the plea. The man understands that he will have to tell the judge what he did. I am dazed by the conversation and the harsh conditions in the jail. When the man stands to leave, he shakes my hand and thanks me for coming to visit him. I find myself surprisingly moved as I make physical contact with an admitted rapist. For the life of me, I cannot hate him or dismiss him. He admits that he has committed a horrible crime against a child. I want to be able to rely on the categories set up in my mind, and I find that I cannot. My eyes tear up instead—for the man, for the victim, and, on some level, for myself. Initial, protective anger stepped aside to allow unexpected vulnerability behind the prison walls.

Another man steps into the room to talk with the lawyer. He is in jail for not supporting his family. Abandonment of women and children is a huge problem that carries a violence of its own. It is a fairly recent legal phenomenon that a man can be put in jail for non-support of his family. Unfortunately, the system is a debtor's prison; with no way to make money beyond selling furniture, the debt continues to grow and there is little hope of resolution or release. The mother and children will continue to live in poverty and the man will likely spend many years in jail with a mounting debt.

While the man is speaking, the first prisoner walks back into the room. He is carrying three bottles of Coke, one for the lawyer, one for the other visitor, and one for myself. He places the Coke bottles on the table and leaves. I drink the warm Coke and listen to a series of men who are in jail for reasons that are objectively crimes. I listen to a few prisoners who are victims of circumstances beyond their control. I am moved again by the hospitality of the poor. I drink from the bottle given me by a man who admits to profound violence against his stepdaughter. I don't particularly enjoy the drink, but under the circumstances I accept it and take into my own body the meaning that it holds. I remember the empty Coke cans on my counter the night a terrified, raped woman appeared at my door. Justice and mercy shall kiss, says Isaiah, and in that process we reach beyond the edges of our own wounds and embrace the mystery of peace. The crimes are true and so is the possibility for redemption. For the victims, for the perpetrators, for the stark lines within my own self-protection, truth and reconciliation with that reality often have their beginnings in small, humanizing acts that in the grace of the moment we choose not to dismiss. The large anger of trauma is domesticated through such small acts and choices. Transformation of energy begins where we stand and gradually becomes passion for the living.

After leaving the jail, we visit a church dedicated to the Virgin of Urkupina. The Virgin of Urkupina appeared after the conquest. The Guadalupe of Bolivia, the image of the Virgin of Urkupina expresses God's knowledge of and presence in the suffering of the people. Mary's presence is a statement that God hears the cries of the people and will not abandon them. Urkupina is a Quechua word meaning "she's up there," referring to the Virgin's presence on the mountain, an earth form held holy in the indigenous people's worldview. She is the mother of the area, the receiver of hopes and prayers and devotion who holds together two different worldviews.

As we enter the church, a nine-day memorial mass is being celebrated. The mourning of the people gathered is expressed in their black clothing and their quiet tears. We slip past the mourners to go into the side chapel filled with candles, flowers, and offerings to the Virgin of Urkupina. In looking around at the signs of faith of a suffering people, I am reminded of the shrines of 9/11. The holy hope flickering in the candles is reminiscent of the divine presence, "she's up there," God is with us, the fact that suffering does not write the last word. I pray then for the prisoner and something in my own soul is suddenly released. I see and experience the moving flame of an internal shift that can have come only from a source other than my own understanding. The spirit of compassion is large enough to embrace all of the contradictions—even if only for a moment, and in an enexpected way.

The release I experienced that day was not of anger at injustice but of the illusion that it was my God-given calling to carry the anger of all victims and make right the suffering of the world. The hospitality of the poor invited me in to dwell in a different truth and find there an appreciation for my own anger and the collapse of ego that indeed brings conversion.

I LEARNED THROUGH A PHYSICAL PROCESS that healing and transformation are cyclical and ongoing. A few days after being cleared to return to work following surgery, the nicely healing wound became warm, painful, and as the surgeon's nurse described it, angry. It was obvious that something had changed and my assumption that I was finished recovering was wrong.

I was upset about having to go back to the surgeon, especially since I thought that I was much further along in the healing process than this newly painful wound would indicate. Diagnosing a suture abscess, the surgeon said, "There is a weakness in the wound so an abscess forms that cannot heal on its own. There has to be an intervention."

Removal of the sutures that were at the source of the infection and ten days of antibiotics solved the problem. And then, long after the second declaration that I was healed, the surgical wound swelled again. "More sutures at a deeper level working their way to the surface," said the surgeon. After the second intervention, the wound quieted down and formed a neat, smooth scar that gives no hint of the unexpected turns in the healing process.

As is clear to me now, that wound knew what it was doing as it swelled and became unexpectedly painful. It was healing its weakness on a deeper level by rejecting what was not of my own body. The weakness in the wound had its own integrity. Compassion for the wound, its angry manifestations and slowness in healing, became fundamental for recognizing that the anger of the abscess was in the service of healing. The anger works out of us what was not ours to begin with; identification of the object of anger externalizes the shame. It must be worked with and taken seriously, no matter how many times its eruption challenges our notions of healing.

The wound has its own integrity and healing process, and it demands respect. The scar tissue left behind is more than a reminder. It is the reference point for a new understanding of life. The scar tissue teaches self-protection. Not everyone in the world can be trusted, but some people can be. Healing is possible, and the ability to know when and how to mobilize appropriate boundaries of self-defense is a major gift of the energy of anger.

FOR TWENTY-SEVEN YEARS before the terrorist attacks in the United States, September 11th had been a day of mourning for the people of Chile. On that day in 1973, Augusto Pinochet led a coup that overthrew a democratically elected president. He and the Chilean military received significant help from the United States in planning and implementing the overthrow and murder of President Salvador Allende. It was a bloody coup that marked the beginning of a long period of pervasive repression and violence. Thousands of Chileans were arrested, tortured, and murdered. Thousands more suffered the loss of loved ones. Poverty was deepened by corruption and people lived in the terror created by the military government.

Remaining in power until 1990, Pinochet has since been charged with murder several times, including by the government of Spain on behalf of Spanish nationals killed during and after the coup. Pinochet, who is without remorse, is a powerful symbol of the military dictatorships that terrorized Latin America in the 1970s and 1980s. Chile's history books were rewritten under Pinochet so that the story of the coup would be told as the salvation of Chile, not the destruction of one of Latin America's most stable democracies. The Pinochet coup reinforced that change through some of the most repressive violence on the continent.

Villa Grimaldi was an isolated mansion at the foot of the Andes. A forty-minute car ride from Santiago, Villa Grimaldi was situated in a beautiful place. It was also a perfectly isolated, yet accessible place to create a interrogation and torture center. It is estimated that more than five thousand people were brought to Villa Grimaldi during the Pinochet years. More than 250 of those people were tortured to death.

Two years before Pinochet stepped down from power and allowed elections, Villa Grimaldi was sold to a developer in a somewhat shady business transaction. The corruption of that real estate deal was exposed, but not before the buildings where the torture occurred had been bulldozed to the ground. Only the ruins were left.

In the years that followed, a former Villa Grimaldi detainee named Pedro Matta, who had returned from exile, fought to have the site turned into a memorial peace park. Torture is meant to destroy spirit and life; it serves no other purpose. Matta interviewed former prisoners and torturers to create a daily record of what had happened at the torture center.

Sadly, some people who had been detained at Villa Grimaldi considered their experience a source of shame, and did not want it to be known that they had been prisoners there. Their hesitancy speaks to the lingering power of torture; even after so much public exposure and discussion of the crimes against humanity, the shame created a captivity of its own. The anger remained directed inward for reasons somehow linked to a mechanism for surviving such a pervasive and total assault. The hope of the public telling of the story is that it will open the possibility of redirecting shame into a social engagement of anger.

Matta helped to mobilize the anger of a wounded nation. He led the movement to reclaim history in a way that honored the suffering of the repression, denounced such abuses through historical consciousness, and restored the beauty of the earth in a place marred by the horrors that had happened there. It was the outrage of the human rights organizations and courageous individuals that made something beautiful in the ruins. The creation of the peace park required and fostered a change in the way that particular space was envisioned. The story and all of the appropriate anger and grief it elicits is told in the presence of a garden: roses among the ruins.

The ruins of individual trauma are transformed by engaging the anger in a way that links one to, rather than separates one from, the rest of humanity. Some form of social engagement of the anger is needed, whether that form be nonverbal, as in commitment to a project or movement that seeks to address prevention of trauma, or verbal, as in a series of conversations in the privacy of a therapist's office. Anger calls for creativity in its expression so that the energy not only will break the silence of trauma, but will be directed to daring to fight like hell for the living. This is the anger that creates a new and safer world.

Dry Bones

From time to time, gravediggers in rural cemeteries strike their shovels against skeletons of infants whose burials were never registered. Heartbroken, the parents may have buried their baby in an adult grave already owned and perhaps even occupied by an aunt or uncle, grandparent or sibling. The addition of the tiny body to the grave was done quietly, and made sense at a time when there were no mourning rituals for the death of an infant.

When the layers of soil are disrupted to bury another body, the bones appear without a story and without a name. Questioning of the family often reveals the identity of the skeleton as someone's child lost at birth. Sometimes the dry bones simply exist on their own, their memory unclaimed, overlooked, or walled off from consciousness. No one knows to whom the bones belong.

The discovery of individual unmarked graves happens more often than one would think. With each unearthing comes knowledge of desperation and heartbreak that led to anonymity. The infant burials break the hearts of those who discover them. Once found, the bones and their implicit stories taken on new life and meaning. The bones and the stories they would tell are brought into the light, and if only temporarily, remembered. For a moment, they live again in the knowledge of the great forces of life that formed them, and the great heaviness of soul that hid them away.

A tragic legacy of the twentieth century is that, since the beginning of World War I, millions of people have simply disappeared into the dust like the bones of the forgotten infants. Across years and worlds there is a marrow-deep ache for the vulnerability of those losses. The deaths and the terror surrounding them have made indelible impressions on those who loved these people and, in a variety of ways, these impressions have haunted their descendants.

All generations, for example, must live with the horrors of the Holocaust. There are flash shadows on building walls that have been preserved in Hiroshima, ghostlike images of the people left behind when the energy of the nuclear blast took a strange photograph as it destroyed bodies. The Mothers of the Plaza de Mayo in Argentina symbolized disappearance, torture, and death in Latin America when week after week they held pictures of their missing children and slowly captured the attention of the world.

The lack of so much as a bone to bury is a pain that lingers from September 11th and other acts of violence. Those who vanished in hunger, in epidemics, and under the grinding heel of poverty are often invisible when human casualties from violence are being calculated. Somewhere their bones lie unclaimed.

The dry bones of these stories have at times been discovered by accident and at other times been carefully excavated as a means of bearing witness and restoring dignity. Sometimes mass graves are found in the pursuit of progress, like the ancient Negro burial ground in lower Manhattan.

The bones were discovered during a federal government construction project. The only trace left of the burial ground had been an early nineteenth-century map with smooth handwriting that indicated the existence of a cemetery for slaves in the very space where it was found. It took a protracted fight to suspend work on the building so that the bones could be gathered.

The bones wanted to tell their stories and their descendants wanted to hear them. The separate nature of the burial ground spoke to the deep prejudice of colonial America and its modern manifestations. A question arose about who owned the bones and who had the right to decide what was to be done with them. The poignancy of that being a point for argument was that even after several centuries, a civil war, and a civil rights movement, the bones of the slaves were still seen in some sectors of society either as unimportant or as objects to be possessed. The discovery of the bones and the controversy surrounding them made clear that the wound of racism is ongoing. Across the harbor from where the Statue of Liberty now stands, people were once bought and sold—and the lessons of that history have yet to be learned.

It took twelve years for the bones to be returned to their burial space. During the interim, scientists read the signs of violence, malnutrition, and early death in the dry bones. These signs told the story of slavery and its brutality. When the bones were reburied in coffins that had been made in Africa, the ceremony was a dignified one that honored memory.

The bones of anonymous slaves and the horrible violence to which they gave testimony were given a place in the conscious history of New York. The story of these slaves began to be told, and it is a process that remains incomplete. The burial ground is now a sacred, but inconspicuous, place. As is the case with many holy sites, one must search to find it among the modern buildings of lower Manhattan's Federal Square. It can be easily overlooked, and it often is.

THE MOURNING RITUALS OF ALL CULTURES require attention to the body as part of the passage into death and rebirth, however that might be defined. The lack of an identifiable body ruptures the act of mourning.

Since 1984, a small group of forensic archeologists from Argentina has overseen the search for the bones that remain from the political violence of the last century. The work of these archeologists began when the military dictatorship in Argentina ended, and the families of thirty thousand people who had disappeared in the "dirty war" cried out for justice.

In the search for the remains of the victims of the repression, dignity was given not only to the people who had died but also to those who mourned them. The exhumations are a key component in documenting human rights violations as a means of preventing such violence in the future. Once bones are found, studied, and identified, they are returned to their families for burial. This difficult search is of vital importance because of the information that it yields, and also because of the opportunity it provides to honor the grieving rituals of the community.

The Argentine Forensic Anthropology Team has traveled the world, helping people to organize the search for their dead. The team works with local people in a four-step process that includes research into the story of what happened and where the bones might likely be found, the digging and excavation that is done by people in search of loved ones, examination and identification of the remains that expose patterns of violence, and reburial. The team has worked in situations where the recovery of bones is so sensitive and dangerous that they have literally slept with the bones to protect them from people who would steal them and carry their meaning away. There is ritual all along the process; such painful work needs to be held in a communal expression of remembrance and hope.

The bones are found because heartbroken people make a decision to search for them, to let light again shine upon them so that their meaning is not lost and grief can finally be given a space to breathe. The Killing Fields in Cambodia, the excavated graves in plain sight from Pinochet's Chile, and bones carefully hidden in Central America all tell their stories. Skulls with bullet holes, hands wired together, broken bones are found in Rwanda, Iraq, and Bosnia. The remains of the victims of violence are re-buried with rituals that complete their life journey. In the North American indigenous understanding, their spirits are no longer bound to the earth.

The earth gives over the bones as testimony to stories that were meant to be kept silent. The stories of the bones bear witness to life and soul, oppression and transcendence. Their testimony brings to light violence that challenges and changes life for those with ears to hear the stories that they have to tell.

It is tempting to keep the bones hidden beneath the busy sidewalks of life; to walk unconsciously on the memory of trauma as if it has nothing left to say to us. Yet in these bones are living memory and the hope that such violence will never happen again. Their stories become the breath of life. For individuals who have suffered trauma that must be kept secret, the dry bones that are isolated and hidden, the stories not told, the emotions not claimed, that breath is foreclosed. When the bones are discovered and their stories are told, the losses are mourned and new life becomes possible for the survivors.

THE PROPHET EZEKIEL WAS A VISIONARY and priest at the time of the Babylonian exile. That exile followed a military siege that destroyed the temple and forced the people of Israel out of the land promised to their ancestors. It was a time when identity and life itself were threatened, a time of heartbreak and alienation from the covenant between God and the people. Jerusalem was in ruins. Ezekiel articulated his vision that the people would return to the land of their birth if they remained faithful to their ancestry. He called his people to live in hope that the fidelity of Yahweh would lead the people back to their homeland.

Ezekiel was led twice by God to Valley of the Dry Bones. During the first encounter with the testimonial bones from the siege, Ezekiel is struck dumb. Perhaps the trauma reflected there is too powerful for words. It has to be observed and absorbed. God urges patience; Ezekiel is to wait and be faithful to his calling until words are given to him. Those words will come as Ezekiel is able to accept them.

Indeed, in time the words are given to Ezekiel, and he speaks them in a way that becomes important for the establishment of Judaism. Ezekiel tells the story of the destruction of Jerusalem while holding firm to the knowledge that there will be a rebirth, even as consciousness of the devastation strains the people's faith.

Having told the story and explained the meaning of the exile, Ezekiel is led back to the valley where, for the second time, he encounters the dry bones of the dead. Yahweh calls Ezekiel to walk among the bones on the floor of the valley, bones as dry as those pulled out of the earth in modern excavations. And those bones have a story to tell. Yahweh asks Ezekiel to prophesy over the bones, to bring God's own breath into their being. Ezekiel utters the prophecy, summoning the winds—the breath of the four directions—and foreshadowing the resurrection in the coming back to life of the dry bones of Israel's hope.

The bones in the valley begin to rattle as the breath is summoned. They become whole again and stand on their feet forming a "vast mutlitude" (Ezekiel 37:10) that represents the promise of wholeness and reconnection to the lost soil of Israel. The bones tell the story of a people separated from the source of life and identity. The dry bones are brought together again to become a new body, a new beginning, to represent a new understanding of who the people of God are called to be.

The individual and communal experience of trauma can be like dry bones hidden in secret places. There may be only fragments of memory, partial skeletons left behind in a part of the self that is struck dumb. The bones can be carried from one generation to the next, separated without story from their place of origin. To prophesy among these bones is to call for a return to their original state, to call the bones together in the power of breath. It is asking the bones to tell their story. It is to grieve what has been lost and believe in the possibility of a future.

The bones left by trauma can be hard to put together, even when there is a powerful desire to heal. When the Israelites left Egypt, they took Joseph's bones with them. Joseph had instructed his descendants not to leave his bones in the land of captivity. The dignity of Joseph's bones lay in his identity not as a slave, but as a child of God. Carrying the bones into the promised land ensured that the history of the people, and their true identity, would never be forgotten.

THE SUMMONING OF THE WIND is finding breath to tell the story of dry bones longing to dance again. Breath is energy. The discipline of breath is a key element of spirituality and it is universally part of prayer. Across religions, breathing brings body and soul into the presence of God. In Judeo-Christian tradition, the breath of God that hovers over the primeval waters creates life and brings about change. The breath of God is the life force—the movement of God within, the creation of a new reality. There is a mighty wind at Pentecost and it frees Jesus' disciples who were huddled in fear to become strong witnesses of faith. In Islam, the taking in of fresh breath means letting God into one's self. The exhalation of breath releases from the body what is not of God. The Sufi believe that every breath inhaled and exhaled that is not done with a conscious connection to the remembrance of God is dead; living breath is that which brings one into the presence of God. The Russian Orthodox Church teaches that the breath can become a conscious prayer through the recitation of a simple petition to God for mercy as one inhales and exhales. Any meditative practice, regardless of its religious origin, depends on deep breathing. Breath is a metaphor for the force within that is both invisible and life sustaining. Breath is the entryway to the soul.

The Hebrew Scriptures use a feminine word, *ru'ah*, to describe breath and spirit. The word also describes the four winds summoned by Ezekiel in his prophecy to the dry bones. *Ru'ah* makes us both spirit and flesh. The word *pneuma* in the New Testament refers to the Holy Spirit promised by Jesus and sent at Pentecost. The Holy Spirit came with a rush of the wind and emboldened the frightened followers of Jesus to tell the gospel story in words that could be understood in the native languages of the listeners. Tongues of fire flowed from the wind. *Pneuma* is also used in the New Testament to describe the spirits of individual persons as well as of evil spirits and demons. So it is that Jesus called the spirits—both good and evil—by name.

Human and divine breath meet in both *ru'ah* and *pneuma*. That breath is deep enough to give life to the bones hidden deep within the soul of the human community and bring them together as an expression of Divine Wisdom.

The Greek translation of the Hebrew Scriptures names the Spirit of Wisdom, the breath of the divine, Sophia. A figure with feminine features, Sophia's image is that of the tender mother, the mirror of energy, the place where the idea of God interacts with our own bodies. It is the spirit that breathes us into being. The breath of God, the Spirit of Wisdom, is capable of holding all elements of trauma. What scholars believe to be one of the last books of the Greek canon describes Sophia as being expansive and compassionate enough to provide breath for even the most dry and abandoned bones.

> There is in her a spirit that is intelligent, holy,
> unique, manifold, subtle,
> mobile, clear, unpolluted,
> distinct, invulnerable, loving the good, keen,
> irresistible,
> beneficent, humane,
> steadfast, sure, free from anxiety,
> all-powerful, overseeing all,
> and penetrating through all spirits

that are intelligent, pure, and altogether subtle.
For wisdom is more mobile than any motion;
because of her pureness she pervades and penetrates
    all things.
For she is a breath of the power of God,
and a pure emanation of the glory of the Almighty;
therefore nothing defiled gains entrance into her.
For she is a reflection of eternal light,
a spotless mirror of the working of God,
and an image of his goodness.
Although she is but one, she can do all things,
and while remaining in herself, she renews all things;
in every generation she passes into holy souls
and makes them friends of God, and prophets;
for God loves nothing so much as the person who
    lives with wisdom.
She is more beautiful than the sun,
and excels every constellation of the stars.
Compared with the light she is found to be superior,
for it is succeeded by the night,
but against wisdom evil does not prevail.

She reaches mightily from one end of the earth to
    the other,
and she orders all things well.
              —Wisdom 7:22–8:1

To breathe into Sophia is to know the power of the soul. The winds summoned by Ezekiel and the life restored in the valley of the dry bones are the breath of Sophia herself, the spirit of Wisdom giving breath to the stories of human life. Sophia as Divine Wisdom presents an image of God within who cannot be damaged by impure realities.

The ability of Sophia to preserve and restore life makes her an ally to those who have experienced trauma.

Breath connects body and soul. Trauma closes off deep breath. The physiological response to trauma has evolved from the need for survival. Temporarily suspending the act of breathing in the face of the shocking marks the first moment of fright before there is an active response to what is overwhelming. Holding one's breath in a traumatic event is part of the physiological response to the threat. The survival instinct to take short, shallow breaths can over time become as suffocating as a premature burial. There may be no conscious awareness of the shallow breaths that are enough to sustain life, but not sufficiently nourishing to bring to life stories that are bone deep. Failing to breathe deeply, failing to find a restorative space where strength can be gathered fuels exhaustion. Breathing, simple as it may seem, can be the holy wind that makes storytelling possible.

Each deep breath drawn by those who have been protecting themselves from trauma or the sense of living in the presence of an ongoing threat is a dramatic leap of faith. The overwhelming feelings evoked by the trauma may be kept in unmarked graves for compelling reasons. To breathe into the feelings is to experience them, which is sometimes too painful to bear. It can be difficult for trauma survivors to breathe the power of memory and testimony without impediment. Traditional methods of meditation are the source of many relaxation processes developed to assist trauma survivors in stabilizing their arousal symptoms.

The first step in universal heart of meditative prayer is to center oneself through focus on the breath. When interrupting thoughts come to mind, they are to be observed, but not judged or resolved. A word, or a mantra, can be helpful in dealing with distracting thoughts. Any word can be chosen. This is not as simple as it sounds. Very few words in the language do not have some type of personal meaning attached to them. Some of the words suggested in the literature will not be immediately appropriate; love may be linked to betrayal, peace may be yoked to an experience of violence, God may be a notion too complex to approach. Intrusive memories are also problematic.

People may find that their chosen methods of prayer fail in the aftermath of traumatic experience. The loss of a spiritual practice increases pain as it seems to block off natural resources for recovery. Breath can be tended in many other ways, the most accessible of which might be physical exercise. For many people, the repetitive movement involved in most forms of physical activity seems to serve the same purpose in the relaxation response as meditation without the disturbance of intrusive memories. The practice of crafts such as knitting and crocheting slow the breath through repetitive action. These simple acts mediated by our bodies and hands can be profound ways to prophesy over our own experience of dry bones.

THERE MUST BE SAFETY for the trauma story to be spoken. Creation of a safe space is facilitated through many different symbolic processes that allow the trauma to be integrated into one's life in a conscious way. Recognizing the many tactile ways in which expression can be given to the trauma story and its accompanying feelings is a key to making the prospect of telling one's story less overwhelming. What is crucial is that someone else receive the story in whatever form it needs to be initially told and retold over time. Remarkable healing takes place through peer groups with people who have had similar experiences, an effective psychotherapeutic relationship, or the presence of a loved one who can serve as witness to the pain. It is not enough to tell the story once in its entirety with the expectation that it never need be told again.

Storytelling is a mosaic carefully constructed from smaller pieces that can be fitted together in different ways, and in ways that do not depend on words alone. Any type of visual representation of the story, or any of its small parts, can be an effective means of recollecting an experience that was overwhelming because of its accompanying sense of powerlessness. Art plays a significant role in healing from trauma because it creates a way of taking what feels overwhelming on the inside and giving it a concrete and finite form. Watercolors done with a child's set of paints can transform what is indescribable verbally into color and form. The instinct to represent experience through even the simplest of drawings is a primal one that has a long history of mediating the effects of trauma.

Particularly helpful is the creation of mandalas. A Sanskrit word meaning "circle," a mandala is a meditative art work that represents wholeness and peace. The circle is a universal symbol of unity that, in one form or another, appears in the worship and social patterns of all cultures and religious traditions. Creation has a circular shape in its most basic form as molecules and cells. The round earth is a circle of life that is constantly renewing itself. Mandalas as a form of meditation are an interaction between the personal life and the cosmos: one life within the reality of all life. An individual mandala exists within the circle of the cosmos.

The mandala can be created in different forms by people of any age. Materials used in mandalas include paper, fabric, paints, and pencils that create patterns and objects within a circle. The mandala emphasizes balance, and can be represented in patterns that are related to different cultures around the world, such as Navajo sand paintings and the rose windows in churches. Carl Jung practiced the meditative act of creating mandalas, which he described as "a safe refuge of inner reconciliation and wholeness." This is art done for the process, not the product, though some of the artwork that emerges can be remarkably evocative and beautiful.

A mandala can be created by anyone. The universality and accessibility of the circle form makes it an excellent way to represent an internal process in an external form. It can be much easier to identify feelings and memories symbolically through the mandala or other art forms than to begin with the creation of a verbal narrative of trauma. The creation of group mandalas has become an important way to share stories as well as to express the hopes and feelings of a group. Several international projects use the creation of a group mandala as a tool of peacemaking and healing; the expression of the individual within the healing circle creates both art and ritual. Mandala making is also a good alternative for relaxation, reclamation, and expansion of breath.

A form of mandala-creation practiced by many cultures is the sand painting. This circular representation of life emphasizes the transitory nature of our own particular lives within the circle of history. The Chinese have a belief that the essential life energy or *chi* permeates all things. This belief in the energy force of life is also consistent across religious traditions. The life force—or what could be called the breath of God—gradually leaves the body in the process of a long death. The differentiated energy that forms the basis of this particular life gradually flows into the larger sea of life. When death is sudden, the differentiated *chi* is "knocked out" of the person, without the gradual process of absorption into the universe. The *chi* that hovers is a hungry ghost; it is misplaced, unremembered, and potentially dangerous. It must be coaxed back into the larger energy of the universe.

For three months following the 9/11 attacks, Tibetan monks silently worked in the large rotunda of the Smithsonian Museum of the American Indian in lower Manhattan. They were engaged in a meditative act, the creation of a large sand mandala on the floor of the museum. The purpose of the mandala was to make concrete and visible the thoughts, memories, and grief of those praying for the victims of the violence. That visibility fed the hungry ghosts by making their presence known. What was overwhelming to the spirit was containable on the floor of the Smithsonian. The mandala emerged over the course of the months, each piece of sand having meaning and beauty that represented both loss of life and hope for the future. On Christmas Eve, the monks swept up the sand and poured it into New York harbor. The thing of beauty created from tiny pieces of the earth was designed to be temporary, a transitional piece that held the process of life poured out and transformed. The *chi* was helped along on its journey, as in other rituals that seek to restore a balance of life. Only then could the energy of life be reborn.

Narrative and Justice

INDIVIDUAL EXPERIENCE OF TRAUMA ALWAYS EXISTS WITHIN a social context. Societal and cultural trauma is expressed in the injuries of each person who is part of the group. Healing of national trauma tends to both the individual and the collective wound. Reconciliation is not possible without that dual purpose.

Perhaps no country was more in need of this type of healing than South Africa at the end of apartheid. A huge, unhealed wound was left behind in the people of South Africa. Transformation of that wound was not automatic or even guaranteed. The poverty, suffering, oppression, torture, death, and institutionalized racism experienced for generations by the black majority was a story that needed to be told. The white minority had benefited from the apartheid system and participated in its perpetuation in terribly damaging ways. This was particularly true of the individuals who served in the security forces.

The trauma of apartheid was a wound so deep that it threatened the stability of the new democracy. There was concern about eruption of a civil war. Globally there is no dearth of examples of the ways in which old wounds lead to new violence. South Africa's 1995 Promotion of National Unity and Reconciliation Act was passed to tend the apartheid wound in the hope that healing and reconciliation might be possible in the country. The government promised amnesty to people on any side of the conflict who had committed crimes against humanity. The condition for the amnesty, however, was that the person who had perpetrated violence needed to testify and make part of the historical record the details of what he or she had done. Victims of violence would also be given an opportunity to testify—often in the presence of the perpetrators—to make their stories part of the record as well.

The Truth and Reconciliation Commission was established by the Government of National Unity to facilitate the amnesty process. This was a new model and it was based on the belief that real reconciliation is possible only when the truth is told. Bishop Desmond Tutu, chairman of the commission, said at its opening gathering in December of 1995, "To be able to forgive, one needs to know whom one is forgiving and why." Later in the address he added, "We are a traumatized people. We all stand in need of healing."

The vision of the Truth and Reconciliation Commission was ambitious and unprecedented. This was not a case of the victors in a war prosecuting the defeated. Rather, the winds of change in South Africa led to a storytelling process where mothers met the people who had killed their children, the tortured met their captors, the security forces met their victims. Individually and nationally, giving breath to the story of the trauma opened up the possibility for new hope.

The Truth and Reconciliation Commission began hearings in April 1996, under the chairmanship of Archbishop Desmond Tutu. Widows, orphans, mothers of victims of the violence wept as they told the story of what had happened to their loved ones. For decades any attempt at change had led to further repression and brutalization. The hearings of the Truth and Reconciliation Commission were held all over South Africa. Stories of true horror emerged, including testimony that the apartheid government at one time sought to develop a bacteria that would kill only blacks. The treatment of blacks in prison was deplorable. Testimony included the story of the beating death of Steven Biko, a black leader who had been reported to have died in an "accident" in prison in 1977. Testimony connected leaders of the white government to church bombings and actions of intimidation. Testimony also implicated the National African Congress in violations of human rights.

The stories were told by people for whom the wound of apartheid was the loss of a loved one, the scars of a beating, the poverty inflicted on the majority. Day after day, in place after place, the Truth and Reconciliation Commission facilitated the storytelling. The people responsible for the violence listened. Sometimes they initially denied the stories that were told, sometimes they openly wept and begged forgiveness.

The brutality of apartheid had been sustained by terror and direct violence. To inflict such violence it was necessary to dehumanize the "other," whether victim or perpetrator. Restoration of a sense of humanity was a powerful experience for those testifying. The Truth and Reconciliation Commission recognized that everyone involved in apartheid and the struggle to end it was a human being. It also created the possibility of compassion for suffering that had largely been kept underground; many had suffered, many had had similar experiences, and few had spoken of them publicly. Breath entered the lungs of people who had been too terrified to speak aloud the horrors of their experience. Terror and isolation began to lose their power.

Not every perpetrator of violence asked for forgiveness and the pain of some victims was so great that some acts of violence remained unforgivable. As Pumla Gobodo-Madikizela, a psychologist who was part of the Truth and Reconciliation Commission, said in her book, *A Human Being Died That Night: A South African Story of Forgiveness,* being able to meet the humanity of the other determines the possibility of forgiveness. When that humanity is not evident, or the evil of events is simply beyond what can be understood and there is no penitence on the part of the perpetrator, forgiveness and reconciliation are not possible. Under such circumstances, it is wrong to press people to forgive their abusers. The hope of authentic forgiveness always originates with the wronged party, who must be able to see the humanity of the other through an acknowledgment of evil.

There can be no excuses offered in this type of truth telling, no comparison to other people's sins, no explaining away the impact of what has happened. The acknowledgment that fosters forgiveness is one that fully claims the destructiveness of actions and events. In the framework of the Truth and Reconciliation Commission, those perpetrators of violence who could claim the evil for what it was could be forgiven. Those who could not, or would not, admit their wrongdoing were granted neither political amnesty nor the forgiveness of the victims.

Basic to the whole process is the fact that truth needs to come from both the victim and the perpetrator. The victim is more likely to speak first, but the acknowledgment of the wrong that was done by the perpetrator must be part of the reconciliation process. This requires an apology without qualification, remorse based on recognition that what happened was wrong. Part of the process of seeking forgiveness is a willingness to make some type of restitution to the victim. The decision to forgive must be made by the victim and cannot be rushed. At the same time, recognition of all of the complexities of a situation where people were forced to behave in ways that were against their basic humanity creates a possibility for reconciliation that stretches beyond a need for retribution.

When victims and families of victims have met with perpetrators, there have been some powerful moments of realization that human beings can commit terrible crimes. To engage in such a dialogue requires the willingness to change that has been a challenge in the Truth and Reconciliation Commission process in South Africa and in subsequent Truth Commissions around the world.

The Truth and Reconciliation Commission gathered facts, documents, and the stories of the people. It gave testimony and reality to the suffering; the bones were found and brought together in a powerful human hope for a new society. Through the honoring of stories, the breath of the truth made reconciliation and a new common life imaginable and gave South Africa the basis for forming a new society. It was recognized that the work of the Commission was only the first step in what would be an ongoing journey in healing the reality of "a traumatized people." Forgiveness was not forced or automatic, but through the telling of truth, the long process of living in the presence of what had happened began to be possible.

THE EXPERIENCE IN SOUTH AFRICA led to the formation of similar Truth Commissions in many countries that have gone through periods of violence and repression. The dry bones of mass graves—many of which were respectfully exhumed by the Argentine Forensic Team—have been part of evidence presented at Truth Commission hearings. El Salvador, Chile, Sierra Leone, East Timor, Bosnia-Herzegovina, and Peru have all had Truth Commission hearings to gather and document the stories of perpetrators and victims in the hope that healing might occur. Commission reports confirm the depth and breadth of pain.

The healing of a nation is a long process that probably requires generations to become fully realized. The process begins with public recognition that the suffering was real. Individual stories touch the common story and find a place of validation. Communal knowledge of what happened replaces isolation and begins the process of mending the social fabric after generations of violence. The underlying principle of the Truth Commission is that the only way to prevent further violence is to claim what has happened and why. The hope born of storytelling and documentation of horrors is that it will be possible for human beings to change the patterns that have led to the violence. This can happen through reconciliation, not only with the horror of the truth but also with the common humanity of all participants in the story.

Recognition of truth and humanity does not erase what has happened or completely heal the injuries of the victim. But it does begin a process of peacemaking, both internally and externally, by shifting an underlying element of violence: dehumanization of the enemy into a symbol of all that is hated and feared. It is easier to kill a symbol than another human being.

Truth Commissions around the world have had their difficulties, many of them rooted in the reality that, unlike the process in South Africa, subsequent Commissions have rarely undertaken their work as part of an amnesty process. Perpetrators of violence have had little incentive to tell the truth, though many have done so as part of their individual process of justice making. It is not easy for people to tell their stories, and to do so reawakens the dry bones of sorrow.

The follow-up to the Truth Commission process in a number of countries has been facilitating grass-roots efforts to help people learn to listen to their neighbors and themselves as they speak of the time of death. Support is needed to live in the presence of their trauma. The commitment to truth often requires consciously living in the company of those who furthered the injuries and violence. Talking and listening with a continued eye on the shared humanity of both victim and perpetrator offer the best hope for living together with integrity.

The most powerful lesson of the Truth and Reconciliation process is that trauma needs to become part of the living story in a conscious way. The wound is part of us, not separate from us. What is true for nations is true for individuals, especially given how often the individual and social narratives are intertwined. The facts of history do not change with the telling of the story. Transformation occurs in the freeing of the energy required to keep the past hidden from view. Forming a narrative is not done in service of bitterness. Rather, it is the concrete expression of hope that the dry bones of one's deepest experience can tell their stories in safety, and thus encounter the Wisdom that leads to rebirth.

The power of history to illuminate the present becomes embodied when the story is told in service of reconciliation. Often the one who must first be reconciled is the person telling the story. To claim what happened among us and within us is a step toward compassion for one's own experience, a compassion that can lead to empathic connection with other human beings. It is not enough to tell the story once with the expectation that its sorrow will immediately depart. The story needs to be told to oneself and to others as part of a reclamation process that leads to a proper burial of what is dead and resolution for the living. Storytelling separates past from present and so creates a new experience of life.

Whether the traumatic story is told as part of a national reconciliation process or in a private setting with the halting phrases of an individual's recounting of events to another person for the first time, giving narrative to the trauma is an important element of healing. Most individuals who have experienced traumatic events will never have the opportunity to tell their story as part of a recognized, organized effort in the service of reconciliation. There might well be no attempt at restitution, or even partial recognition on the part of the perpetrators that violence or grief has occurred. Direct confrontation of perpetrators may be dangerous or ill advised. However, telling one's story does not necessarily require that type of confrontation. It is a matter of giving breath to the truth of powerful and traumatic experience in some forum that externalizes internal experience. Giving breath to an individual story requires courage and ongoing choice.

Recognizing the powerful impact of one's experience does not necessarily end the pain. It does, however, create the possibility for releasing the energy required to keep the silence. One of the most difficult concepts to incorporate in language learning is tense: how to separate what has happened from what one was afraid would happen, how to differentiate past, present, and future. Initially, the trauma narrative knows only the present tense. Telling the story in a way that brings words and emotion into the same sentences requires a language learned through practice. It is through this process that the past becomes differentiated from the present and the possibility of future hope can be articulated.

Often enough in trauma, the first person who must be forgiven is oneself; the trauma survivor carries a multitude of perceived sins, including survival itself. To know one's own story—without qualifications—is to liberate oneself from blame and hopelessness The trauma that has held the center of consciousness becomes one part of a larger story as the focus of life begins to shift toward social engagement. Freud described this release of energy as "Where it was, I shall become."

Making Memorials

THERE IS A STRANGE PROBLEM IN WASHINGTON, D.C. So many memorials have been built in the nation's capital that there is a paucity of space to create more of them. Some discussion has been undertaken regarding the possibility of recycling pedestals and public spaces that currently honor people and actions that seem to no longer have significance worthy of a formal memorial.

One of the figures whose statue may be replaced is that of the Army officer whose role in the Civil War was to keep Ulysses S. Grant sober. Though Grant did slip from time to time—particularly in periods of boredom when he mourned his separation from Mrs. Grant—he was sober in the battles, where it counted the most. The officer's accomplishments most likely did have an impact on the outcome of the war. They certainly contained an element of heroism.

Nonetheless, his memorial space is being threatened by admirers of heroes of more recent memory, people who want to relegate such lesser-known brave ones to footnotes and warehouses. The vacated pedestal would then be available to hold a new memorial statue. The ongoing discussion about all this demonstrates how public memory is often managed by political processes and pressures, and how, with time, unacknowledged memory can lose its meaning.

How do survivors of private and public trauma construct a memorial to their suffering and remarkable resilience? A memorial of trauma is not made of granite. It is created out of the materials of daily life. We live in the presence of sacramental expressions of memory, expressions constructed of small things. The personal items left in front of the Vietnam War memorial create a second level of remembering; the personal interacting with the communal mourning.

My own yard is something of a memorial forest. There is the tree that we planted when our neighbor died suddenly and at too young an age. There are the white pines, a symbol of peace for many indigenous people, planted in memory of friends working in the violence of the Sudan. And there is the tree that my husband quietly planted on September 12, 2001, as a living reminder. Each of these memorial trees has its meaning and helps us call to mind the hope of rebirth, even in the midst of loss. Planting flower beds and trees has long served as a means of living memorial.

A unique way of making a memorial to all of the victims of trauma occurred in Guatemala through the REHMI project. REHMI is the Spanish acronym for the Recovery of Historical Memory. Guatemala has suffered four decades of genocidal violence. Most of the violence was inflicted on the native Mayan people. When peace accords were signed in 1995, there was a call for reconciliation of the peoples of Guatemala. However, no mechanism was put in place to receive the stories of the traumatized people.

During the years of violence, the Catholic Church at great risk had borne witness to what was happening in Guatemala, documenting the torture and killings at a time when to do so was to risk one's life. Now the church was prepared to sponsor a structured, grass-roots project that would give voice to people who had been terrorized and silenced for generations.

The intent of REHMI was to record and honor the memory of the people who had suffered crimes against humanity. It differed from South Africa's Truth and Reconciliation Commission in that amnesty was not part of the process. The fundamental goal of REHMI was to create a memorial to those who had suffered from the genocide. Collecting the stories of the people in a type of memorial process would honor the loss and courage of a people much sinned against by making certain that what had happened to them would never be forgotten.

The REHMI process began with a yearlong program to educate people about the need for collecting the stories. The memories had been forced into a silence that had led to serious health consequences, including depression, headaches, nervous system problems, and nightmares. The healing metaphor used by REMHI was the water jug that is commonly used in Guatemala. An intact jug represented the community before the violence had occurred. A broken jug symbolized the community after the violence. The water jug became a powerful symbol of the desire to make the community whole again by bringing together the broken pieces of each story of violence and loss.

REMHI unfolded within the context of the liturgical year, with the scriptures of each Sunday being explicitly linked to the recovery of historical memory. The placement of the process within the faith life of the community kept the people in touch with their deepest traditions, even as the horror of the genocide was explored.

REMHI was called a Pentecost for the country, a new spirit of hope that honored the identity of the Mayan people. All were invited to tell their stories in their native tongue; the Mayan people speak twenty-seven different languages. Most of the violence in Guatemala was done to the Mayan people. To survive, the Mayan people had to abandon their villages and traditions and go underground with their cultural identity because it marked them for death. Speaking aloud in their language was a dangerous undertaking. Native dress was given up to avoid immediate identification as Mayan. Honoring the story of the Mayan people by having it told in their own language was indeed a new awakening of the spirit. It was an acknowledgment that the lives and the culture of a people much sinned against were worthy of being remembered and honored.

In meetings in churches, small homes, and other places considered safe, testimony was taken from more than seven thousand people. The REHMI interviews were structured to gather empirical evidence about the violence that had occurred. Each story told of villages destroyed, pointing to a systematic pattern of violence intended to eliminate the Mayan people.

One of the most devastating—and invisible—crimes against the people was rape of the women. REMHI became a unique memorial to the suffering of women whose shame kept them further isolated in what was a hideous situation. The raped women of Guatemala spoke of their violation with tremendous courage. Their stories were joined to the stories of women around the world whose rape is only now being considered by the international community as a war crime.

When people were killed, the norm was that there were no bodies for burial. This ruptured the Mayan view of the cycle of life and death. Violent destruction of the earth, the source of life, was also brutal violence against a people whose cosmology includes reverence for the earth. Through the creation of the memorial, the deep resource of the people's cosmology was not only accessed but also made whole as it was called on to restore the meaning of life. Mayan and Catholic priests stood together in the rituals that remembered and honored the dead.

Historical memory was recovered by the courageous recovery and documentation of stories told at great risk. The data from the interviews was collected, analyzed, and published in a four-volume set with a sadly familiar title: *Nunca Mas*—Never Again. The dissemination of the material back to the people of Guatemala was seen as a crucial step in putting the shattered water jug back together. The cracks in the jug held the memory of the violence, while its reconstruction was a starting point for reconciliation and reconstruction.

Creative models of community mental health were developed to help people deal with the emotions awakened by the REHMI process. Those models include engaging in rituals of mourning, teaching physical stabilization techniques, and working with common symbols in the culture as ways of expressing what had come to simply be called *la tristeza*—the sadness. It is finally possible to remember and mourn the dead in public.

The words recorded in Deuteronomy 30:19 as "Today . . . I have set before you life and death, blessings and curses. Choose life so that you and your descendants may live" were spoken by Moses in a transitional moment when it had become clear that, though he had wandered the desert, he would not live to see the promised land. Moses recounted the memory of the exodus to remind his tired people of who they were and where they had come from, and the potential of that complex memory to lead them to their homeland. The memory of their struggle and journey could fuel bitterness and separation, or it could live as a source of compassion and hope based on the fidelity of God. A wanderer in the wildness of the wound learns that fidelity to memory is a matter of living day to day with consciousness and attentiveness to one's own reality while remembering the presence of God. The journey toward wholeness is nourished by the memory of manna harvested close to the ground.

THE PROCESS OF HONORING MEMORY confronts us with the realization that there are limits to what can be changed or brought into being, even through the best-intentioned efforts. That experience brings the helper/witness back into the heart of the helplessness of trauma, the inability to affect a change in outcome. But from that deep sense of failure comes the realization that to be a witness to trauma requires nothing less than surrender to the fundamental truths of human life.

We who are limited live in the immanent presence of a transcendent God. What we cannot do for others causes grief that is linked to new imagination. Presence to the pain of another does not require that we provide a solution. Rather, it means holding the memory of each person's suffering and transformation as sacred. Witnesses to trauma need to be willing to continually cycle through the process of healing; to move, to breathe, to give expression, to find social support.

Called by different names in the literature, compassion fatigue affects those who witness the sufferings of others. The empathic connection required to serve as a witness also holds the potential to stir up one's own losses and unresolved grief. It has been documented that those who witness the trauma of another experience the same biochemical changes as the person directly experiencing the trauma. The effect is even more profound if the trauma is experienced by a loved one.

That trauma is contagious in some way does not suggest that contact with people living through trauma or its aftermath of grief should be avoided. Rather, it is to acknowledge that we are never neutral observers of life, particularly in life situations that cry out for justice or remedy. The implications of the research are experientially known by people working in human service professions. Great care must be taken of oneself, as well as of the other. There needs to be some mechanism for processing one's own traumatic reactions, experiences, and frustrations. Professional and personal support is imperative for people whose choice is to be a compassionate witness. It is a difficult journey that simply cannot be undertaken on the power of one's own commitment or desires.

Living with consciousness of the reality and impact of trauma demands attention to the feelings evoked by the other person's trauma. Trauma survivors do not need the additional complication of someone else's experience being projected onto their own. Teamwork and a network of social support is required if the witness is to remain authentic and capable of the empathic connection so vital in a compassionate relationship.

Those who have to be able to meet the needs of a deeply wounded person delude themselves if they think that they can do it without paying a personal price. If nothing else, being a witness to suffering significantly changes one's point of view. It is necessary to maintain a balance that holds the reality of suffering in one open hand and the possibility and experience of joy in the other. The same processes of reducing stress and breathing into one's own experience of trauma are required of the witness. Permission is necessary to grieve one's own losses, even if they seem inconsequential in comparison to the pain of others. Comparison of pain is never a fair exercise, because it can serve to deaden and discount one's own experience without alleviating the suffering of the other. Yes, people around me may have suffered more, but I hurt as well. Judging that pain insignificant or pushing it away from consciousness can be a powerful form of denial. The result is a hardening of the heart.

During an interview with an international worker charged with responsibility for famine relief, I asked the question "How does this work affect you?" He replied that it didn't affect him at all because he kept a professional distance that was protective. As he described that distance, it became very apparent that whatever connection he had made with the people had been quietly severed. He saw them completely as outside of him and their suffering did not move him. Or so he believed. Relationships in other areas of his life were impoverished as a result of a persistent, low-grade depression that he dismissed as unrelated to his work. It took months for him to even be open to the possibility that he was experiencing vicarious trauma. A huge piece of the resistance was the recurrent theme in trauma that his symptoms were the result of a failure to keep sufficient distance, to differentiate at all times his suffering from that of other people.

It is not disloyal for people who work and live in the presence of terrible suffering to laugh and enjoy life. One of the initial curiosities for those who spend a significant time in developing countries is how people can retain a spirit of celebration in the presence of their ongoing grief. At first glance, the continuation of a tradition of celebration has been mislabeled as denial. Many communities in Peru that were surrounded by the violence of Shining Path guerillas and the military response of counter-terrorism survived the violence and grief in part because the communities never cancelled a meeting, celebration, or other gathering, regardless of what was happening in the area or the fear provoked by the violence. The people never let the terror take away their dancing. The resulting sense of community, coupled with the physical, emotional, and spiritual release of the ritual and dance itself, was protective. The ability to continue dancing not only creates a counterbalance to persistent suffering, but also keeps a social system intact.

Symptoms of trauma and grief that come from being present to others are not something less than the suffering that has been observed. Rather, they are part of the human connection that has been made and thus need to be respected in their own right. A common response to the trauma of others is to work harder in the hope that all the wrongs of life can be righted through one's own efforts. The inevitable failure of those efforts only compounds a sense of worthlessness and exhaustion.

It is in that experience of emptiness, frustration, and loss of meaning that the unconscious makes itself known. What we might be attempting to heal in ourselves through work with others becomes clearer; there is always a connection between our own stories and the lives of those we seek to accompany or assist. Rather than seeing that connection as somehow invalidating work done on behalf of others, it is my belief that the relationship between one's own experience and the ability to be empathic to the truth of another person is a holy thing. When we witness and receive the suffering of others, we are standing on a sacred and common ground where listening carefully teaches us about the meaning of our own experience and the reality of the human condition. We sometimes learn the most about the mystery of being alive by staying close to realities of death and limitation. The lessons taught by that mystery call us to the deepest transformations of all.

A New Heaven
and a New Earth

ALL LANGUAGE LEARNING INVOLVES WHAT LINGUISTS CALL "the silent period." During this time the child retreats and silently plays. No words can be coaxed from the child as the moments of silence consolidate what has been learned and lay the groundwork for future, more complex expression.

To heal from trauma is to make meaning of the experience by finding some form of language that holds its truth. The ability to give voice to the trauma experience and its meaning frequently requires a silent period when the process is working on a deep level. During those moments, the seeming loss of words is actually restorative. The process calls for play, a time that lets the truth sift through the deepest levels and find its own patterns of expression.

Images and symbols emerge from the silent grieving period with transformative power. Sometimes those images serve as a reminder that conversion is often the reversal of an earlier understanding of reality, the other side of what had been previously accepted as truth.

Trauma causes an encounter with truth that invites movement toward a spirituality beyond words, familiar concepts, and borders. The power of the individual wound is its capacity to give birth to compassion. This is a spirituality of holding our truths as powerfully—and perhaps for a time in as great a hidden, mysterious darkness—as an unborn child. When known language and understandings cannot hold the wound, and may in fact deepen it, new symbols and images are required for the sacred process of healing.

To see the face of God in trauma requires that we sometimes visit places where we would prefer not to go. One of the most difficult passages is recognition of the poverty of our images of God to explain the mystery of suffering, take it away, or at times, even offer much in the way of comfort.

We all carry images of God in our hearts and minds, incomplete images affected by personal and collective history, gender, and the ability of the image to hold our longings for communion. Common images of God appear in Western art: the good shepherd, creation stirred by the Holy Spirit, God the father, God the judge, God the source of love. Jesus has been represented in many forms that often mirror the culture that is giving him form. There is blond/blue-eyed Jesus, the barefoot Jesus of Native Americans, Jesus the Middle-Eastern Jewish man, the laughing Jesus, the suffering Jesus.

Surrender to anything or anyone—including God as we may experience God—has inherent difficulties for someone who has been overcome by the violence of another. Traditional notions such as obedience to the will of God are fraught with tension when one's own will has been violated. Losing a sense of who God is in our lives, or the means of access to God, or in the darkest moments of pain experiencing a seemingly total absence of God, is part of the transformation that occurs in the wake of trauma.

In the twelfth century Meister Eckhart said that "the ultimate leave taking is to go from God to God." Eckhart was referring to the reality that God, like the expanding cosmos, cannot be contained within the limits of human imagination, language, or ability to explain. Even in experiences of total communion with God, we are left with no words, images, symbols to capture incomprehensible mystery, wonder, and love. We cannot completely know the fullness of God; at best we look in the glass darkly.

Our deepest feeling of connection with God is usually fleeting. Teresa of Avila once said that her most profound and mystical experiences of God lasted less than a half hour and that she was sustained by the memory of the union for years, especially in her darkest moments. The whole of her longing was based on those brief moments of encounter that let her know the presence of God beyond all telling. And Teresa, like the mystics before and after her, never claimed to have experienced the fullness of God's mystery.

Eckhart's description of leave taking captures the experience of loss that occurs with the transition from one experience of God to another. When we realize our own limitation in knowing the whole of God, when prayer becomes dry or our operant image of God loses its ability to hold our life experience, there is a feeling of profound loss. Something meaningful is left behind and there is no immediate replacement in sight. The suffering of that loss is particularly acute if it comes at a time when other aspects of life are in turmoil. One experience of God must be surrendered so that we may enter more deeply into the mystery of a God who is beyond our understanding. There can be a long period of transition between those ways of knowing, a time filled with a feeling of great abandonment and doubt. For those who have experienced trauma, the spiritual transition period often occurs after the events have passed. People have described to me a felt sense that God was with them in the moment of the trauma itself. The pain of transition comes in trying to reconcile the memory of that reality with previous concepts, images, or experiences of God.

The psalms tell us that the question "Where is God now?" is as ancient as the human experience of despair. The scriptures of lament hold a key for understanding the passage between one experience of God and another, particularly when the passage is associated with trauma. The most powerful hunger for God is known in the feeling of seeming absence. The lament is, at heart, a profession of faith. It is the cry of the soul to be held by a presence deeper than the pain.

Our souls are strong enough to embrace even the apparent loss of God. The soul is the integrating wholeness of the human and the divine. The soul is where we make our deepest interpretations of life and experience connection with our God. The powerful reality of love brings all things together into a unity that is larger than any individual element; it is the receiving soul. It is the place where God lives and writes. Sometimes we may know only the traces of that writing, yet its existence in our soul is everlasting. We create ritual using the power of natural elements—the water of purification and baptism, the fire of candles and transforming anger, nourishing wheat from the earth and our inner garden, breath that celebrates the powerful winds of life that change us.

Our spirit holds and celebrates continuity with its ancestors—the communion of saints—and all living things. The soul is given to mysteries and symbols. It receives God's spirit and gives us the power of transcendence. The deepest knowledge resides there; to know in one's soul is to be in the presence of the undeniable. The soul is where healing from trauma happens in its own rhythm and time. The soul is big enough to hold pain and deep enough to nurture courage. There we live and experience trauma, not as our own solitary horror but as part of human communion.

The image reflecting the pain caused by others can be so deep that it threatens or symbolically kills the power of the soul to bring the truth together and find its sacred meaning. Yet the soul can never be completely extinguished, even if we know only the pain that tells us we have been injured and the longing to be healed. The soul originates in God, and God cannot be destroyed. The life source of the soul is eternal compassion, because the soul is the home of divine life itself. There is pain in life that is powerful enough to shake belief and access to the soul. Yet the notion of the soul ultimately being indestructible crosses cultures and religious traditions. Even the wounded soul retains a desire to live.

The transition period between a previous experience of God and one that is congruent with trauma often seems silent and empty. This is the silence of gestation, not of isolation and secrecy. No language, no concept is adequate, but deep integration of learning is at work. A symbol of the silent period in spirituality is the illumination of the five-thousand-year-old New Grange tombs in Ireland. The largest of these tombs is filled with light only on the winter solstice; the darkest day of the year has an angle of illumination that fills the place of death with the brightest sunlight. In a manner reminiscent of St. Teresa, the memory of the light is sufficient to engender hope until it is seen and experienced again. The waiting for that experience may be long, arduous, and filled with grief. This is the experience that has been written about through the centuries under different names: the spiritual impasse, the dark night of the senses, the transitional space, and the cloud of unknowing.

The seeming loss of God is, in actuality, a passage into a deeper relationship with the God who is beyond our projections, images, or understanding. This is the God of trauma, the God for whom sharing in the suffering of humanity is the primary expression of love. The pathway to God as the ground of our being is one that requires loss of the familiar and a tolerance for both ambiguity and the dark energy that, according to scientists, holds the universe together. This is the energy of loss and rebirth, the suffering of one's own reality, and the grace of knowing that along the way of this leave taking, we all drink from the weeping stone.

For the trauma survivor, this reversal means a recognition that what saved one's life is worth treating with reverence, even if the continued symptoms cause distress. The loss of the image of a protective God carries with it the experience of presence in the midst of the human reality of suffering. The memories that are so carefully avoided also carry within them the capacity for understanding and human connection. They are the cornerstones of hope. What would be discarded and cast from consciousness is, in reality, flesh-and-blood experience of the lowly being raised up, the hungry soul satisfied with good things, the promise of redemption fulfilled. Survival is worth the trouble. A love that takes in all of those realities is written upon the soul as its center, a deep well that can transform all the contradictions of trauma, its feelings and its dreadful knowledge, into the energy of life.

The intellectual understanding or familiar image of God is challenged by trauma. The embodied experience of God must lead the journey toward healing; this is the God whose presence is known in the moment of trial without image or words.

THE VILLAGE HYSTERIC OF HISTORY was often the woman who could see the truth in the world around her. Making that truth known caused her to be cast out of the mainstream, marginalized, with the expression of her truth judged as the harbinger of her weakness. *Hyster,* the Greek root word of "hysteric," means womb. Hysteria was thus thought to be linked directly to the feminine organs, which were already suspect because of the blood taboo. Hysteria, in some contexts, meant that the womb had slipped away from the tendons that hold it in place. The womb then wandered about the body and became lost.

That wandering uterus expressed itself through the emotional symptoms of women whose traumatic stories were ignored by a system that could not acknowledge or embrace their reality. That the women wept, cried, fainted, had confusing memories, and told horrible stories was further evidence that they could not be trusted. The sick or wandering uterus caused the women to act irrationally. Those symptoms were believed to be essentially female since men lacked the problematic organ whose unpredictability and instability could cause such chaos. Hence they could not show signs of hysteria, though we now know that, for men, the same symptoms were simply called by different names.

The hysteric is easy to dismiss, particularly if the relationship between symptoms and experience is broken. When separated from their cause, the appropriate trauma responses seem to be madness that is not to be taken seriously. The presence of any womb, let alone one that has wandered and caused all these symptoms, was seen as categorically problematic. That the womb is the source of new life is lost in the historical propensity to link its fecundity with a perception of madness.

The Hebrew word for compassion is *rahamin;* its root word is *raha,* which means womb. *Rahamin,* the compassionate womb, refers to the expression of the highest human virtues. Compassion is stirred by the reality of one's own suffering and that of others. A connection is made between two hearts and both parties are changed. The womb of *rahamin* does not wander, but is steady in its identity as the carrier of life. To be compassionate is to birth transformation. The womb nurtures, it responds, it holds the potential for new creation. *Rahamin* is firmly in place. It is sometimes described as the compassionate womb of God, the manifestation of divine love. *Rahamin* tenderly holds the stories of trauma and transforms the wounds into a rich understanding of life's limits as well as its wonders. *Rahamin* is the place to rest, to gather courage, and to reconnect with the source of life. To believe in *rahamin* is to experience the power of a compassionate witness to our suffering; God sees, God knows our sorrow, God draws us to God's center. *Rahamin* gives birth to the kind of hope that led Moses through the desert.

Though the compassionate womb may seem hidden and at first glance appear inaccessible, its invitation is experienced in the desire to live in spite of overwhelming circumstances. *Rahamin* is capable of holding the holy silent periods of trauma and of giving breath for speaking one's truth. No matter what process or modality is part of the experience of integrating trauma, without the compassionate womb, meaning cannot be fully constructed.

The experience of compassion brings us in touch with the very life force of God, the strength to dance and weep.

Rahamin is known in our souls. *Rahamin* can tolerate and transform the sin of the world. As that evil is known in individual hearts and in the suffering of the world, God as the womb of compassion knows the truth of the distressing stories and gives birth to peace. To live in *rahamin* is to know the potential energy of human suffering, not as an abstract and beautiful idea, but as an embodied reality that transforms the isolation of trauma into the communion of the saints. *Rahamin* is transformation at the very root of our understanding and perceptions. The truth of suffering, its complexities, contradictions, and doubts, are tenderly held by God.

THE JUDEO-CHRISTIAN STORY is rooted in the trauma and memory of separation that occurred when humans first attempted to gain the knowledge of God. The trauma in Genesis is the separation that knowledge brings—being expelled from the wholeness of the garden because of reaching for forbidden knowledge. Much of trauma involves forbidden knowledge. Living with the knowledge of what human beings can do to each other—whether witnessed or directly experienced—creates an exile from the idea of a perfect garden untouched by evil or suffering. Such knowledge creates a change in one's being.

Healing is not a matter of exorcizing knowledge and returning to a lost sense of innocence, but rather a process of embracing the wound and all of its implications. Possessing the knowledge of good and evil often means that we have to change in some way to accommodate the strain on our hearts. Most certainly, both our self-image and our worldview are pushed beyond well-known boundaries. When we come into the world where good and evil are continually held in contrast to each other and yet are linked in their co-existence, the image of God as only the keeper of the garden is challenged. Knowing about the wonder of the garden and the horror of human suffering is a human burden that is carried through personal and collective history.

Captivity in Egypt, wandering in the wilderness, the destruction of the temple, the experience of exile, and ultimately the death and resurrection of Christ are stories of the trauma of a people. Within the larger story, we meet the individual people whose lives carry the wound of their people. Moses was placed in the reeds by his mother, whose own heart broke as she saved her son's life. Having been raised in the Pharaoh's household, Moses recognized who he was when he saw the overseer beat an Israelite. Moses claimed his identity and then, as a result of that connection, was able to return to the trauma of his people and become a leader.

Moses meets God in the burning bush—the I AM of a passion that fuels but does not consume, the fire in the sky by night to lead through the desert, the sacred ground. Moses covers his face and is afraid to look at the manifestation of God, even as God speaks with compassion for the suffering of the people. With that encounter, Moses begins a series of conversations with God that empower him to ask Pharaoh to release the slaves.

The reality of presence, being, I AM, the fire, the passion, and continuity through the seasons of life is a direct expression and experience of the divine, the passion that illuminates also hears the cries of the people. Healing miracles have a way of revealing themselves through the day-to-day in ways that cannot be stored. The openings for conversion of oneself and the world must be part of each day. Through our embrace of life's wounds, each of us can offer others our tiny bit of manna for the journey toward wholeness.

None of us can create the promised land where there will be no more suffering or sorrow. Still, within the wound there is the capacity for hope for nothing less than communion with the mysteriously compassionate and wounded God. After trauma, we long for both a new heaven and a new earth. We find it as we join with others to make a difference, to reach out, to let the truth of the world come to our doors. The nature of God's wound is the passionate fire of living memory; the I AM of human history. It is the energy of transformation.

Also by Teresa Rhodes McGee

Jim's Last Summer
Lessons on Living from a Dying Priest
ISBN 1-57075-420-9

WINNER OF THE CHRISTOPHER AWARD!

The true story of a young woman's friendship with a dying priest, and the life-enhancing gifts they gave to each other.

Ordinary Mysteries
Rediscovering the Rosary
ISBN 1-57075-363-6

Practical and inspirational, this book offers contemporary meditations on the fifteen mysteries of the Rosary, and a simple how-to for those unfamiliar with this ancient way of prayer.

Please support your local bookstore, or call 1-800-258-5838.
For a free catalogue, please write us at
Orbis Books, Box 308
Maryknoll NY 10545-0308
or visit our website at www.orbisbooks.com

Thank you for reading *Transforming Trauma*.
We hope you enjoyed it.